War of 1812

COMBAT

US Soldier

VERSUS

British Soldier

Gregg Adams

Illustrated by Johnny Shumate

OSPREY PUBLISHING
Bloomsbury Publishing Plc
Kemp House, Chawley Park, Cumnor Hill, Oxford OX2 9PH, UK
1385 Broadway, 5th Floor, New York, NY 10018, USA
E-mail: info@ospreypublishing.com
www.ospreypublishing.com

OSPREY is a trademark of Osprey Publishing Ltd

First published in Great Britain in 2021

A catalog record for this book is available from the British Library.

ISBN: PB 9781472841674; eBook 9781472841681;
ePDF 9781472841650; XML 9781472841667

21 22 23 24 25   10 9 8 7 6 5 4 3 2 1

Maps by www.bounford.com
Index by Rob Munro
Typeset by PDQ Digital Media Solutions, Bungay, UK
Printed and bound in India by Replika Press Private Ltd.

Osprey Publishing supports the Woodland Trust, the UK's leading
woodland conservation charity.

To find out more about our authors and books visit
www.ospreypublishing.com. Here you will find extracts, author
interviews, details of forthcoming events and the option to sign up for
our newsletter.

Acknowledgments

The author wishes to thank the following organizations for use of their
images in this book: Getty Images; the Anne S.K. Brown Military
Collection (Brown University Library); the McCord Museum (Canada);
the NRA Firearms Museum; and the Royal Armouries. He would also
like to acknowledge his editor at Osprey Publishing, Nick Reynolds.
Without Nick's advice, help, and patience, this book would not have
been possible.

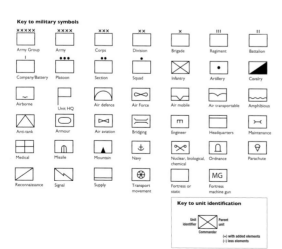

CONTENTS

Introduction

The causes of the War of 1812 (1812–15) are still debated by historians today. Two issues underlie any explanation; Britain's worldwide war against Revolutionary and Napoleonic France and policies that supported Indian opposition to settlement on the American western frontier. Britain blockaded commerce to and from France as part of its war strategy, which resulted in the Royal Navy seizing many American merchant ships on the high seas. Coupled with impressment of American seamen to serve in the manpower-hungry Royal Navy, these actions caused increasing American anger and rising tensions. "Free Trade and Sailors' Rights" became a slogan expressing many Americans' views on why it was thought right to fight the British. On the frontier, the British traded with Indians and provided weapons. Some of these Indians went on to raid American farms and settlements, which caused many to view a war and the elimination of the British Indian trade as the solution to the "Indian problem." Although the United States was not prepared for any conflict, the US Congress declared war on Britain June 18, 1812.

Historians have divided the land war into the Canadian theater (1812–15), the Creek War (1813–14), the Chesapeake Bay campaign (1813–14), and the Gulf of Mexico theater (1813–15). The Canadian theater encompassed the Old Northwest (Michigan, Ohio, Indiana), the Niagara River, the St. Lawrence River, and the Lake Champlain valley. In the Old Northwest there were never more than a few hundred regulars present. Here the fighting was mainly skirmishing and guerrilla warfare between British-allied Indians, supported by a few companies of redcoats, and US troops who were mainly frontier militiamen from Ohio and Kentucky. The Niagara River border saw most of the major battles between regulars. Other than a failed American advance against Montreal in fall 1813, which ended in a fiasco, the St. Lawrence and Champlain regions saw little action. The Creek War was fought in parts of what are now the states of Georgia, Alabama, and Mississippi. The combatants were primarily Creek Indians supplied with weapons and powder by British

The battle of Tippecanoe, November 7, 1811, was an Indian defeat. Between 1783 and 1812, many Americans believed the British were behind Indian attacks upon frontier settlements and travelers. Captured British trade goods, including muskets, confirmed the frontier's belief that the British must be expelled from Canada for safety. (Library of Congress, LC-DIG-pga-01891)

traders, against American regulars and militiamen supported by Indian allies hostile to the Creeks. The Chesapeake Bay campaign was the result of British amphibious raids involving a large contingent of British regulars in 1814. The Gulf of Mexico theater also saw British amphibious strikes and US offensives aimed at capturing or neutralizing British posts supplying the Creeks and other Indians. Here too, the frontier states' militias provided the bulk of US forces.

The war in the Canadian theater started with the Americans slowly assembling troops along the Niagara River and near Lake Champlain while a third force, called the Northwest Army, concentrated at Detroit in the Michigan Territory. Many Americans believed that the conquest of Canada was "a mere matter of marching," in the words of Thomas Jefferson. What these people did not comprehend was that the presence of British regulars, the quality of the Canadian militia, and the opposition of most Canadians to any thought of becoming part of the United States meant any invasion would be fiercely resisted.

Control of Lakes Ontario and Erie was critical and each side built large naval squadrons on the lakes. On Lake Ontario the navies' leadership was cautious and each avoided battle, resulting in neither side gaining control of that lake. In contrast, the US Navy squadron's victory on Lake Erie in 1813 caused the British to withdraw from Detroit and western Upper Canada. (Library of Congress, LCCN 2004662394)

The St. Lawrence River and Lakes Ontario and Erie served as the primary British supply line west of Quebec and Montreal. River and lake vessels plied these waters, bringing reinforcements and needed supplies to the British Army, civilians, and Indian allies. The main US supply line went by river and overland tracks from the Hudson River Valley in New York to Oswego on Lake Ontario. Transport was then by boat and ship to Four-Mile Creek near Fort Niagara or to Sackett's Harbor. Both sides started building naval squadrons on Lake Ontario to control the lake and support their armies. The main British naval station and shipyard was located at Kingston and the Americans' at Sackett's Harbor.

The Niagara River region became hotly contested because an invasion by river crossing was an easier task to accomplish than conducting an amphibious operation across Lake Ontario. In 1812 the first US attack across the Niagara resulted in an embarrassing defeat for the invaders at Queenston Heights. In 1813 and 1814 each side conducted raids across Lake Ontario that included amphibious landings, but none of these was intended to occupy territory permanently. The main US offensive in 1813 was carried out by Major General James Wilkinson in November. This attack, using boats to transport US forces down the St. Lawrence River, was aimed at capturing Montreal. The US forces were defeated by a smaller British force at Crysler's Farm and retreated to French Mills, New York, for the winter. In 1814, under new and aggressive leadership, US forces crossed the Niagara, captured Fort Erie, and participated in battles at Chippawa and Lundy's Lane that fought the British to a stalemate.

The first actions of 1812 in the Canadian theater were in the Old Northwest. These went badly for the Americans. The British speedily assembled a force of 300 regulars, 400 militiamen, and 600 Indians near Detroit and went on the offense. After his troops suffered defeats in several skirmishes, the American commander, Brigadier General William Hull, became fearful of an Indian massacre. When informed by the British commander, Major-General Isaac Brock, that the Indians could not be controlled, Hull agreed to surrender. On August 16, 1812, the American Northwest Army of 2,100 men, including 1,600 Ohio state militiamen, capitulated in and around Detroit to the smaller British force. The frontier was soon subjected to Indian raids, and American positions at Fort Dearborn (Chicago, Illinois) and Fort Mackinac (Michigan) were lost to Indian attacks. Other raiding parties struck settlements throughout the Indiana, Illinois, and Iowa territories.

Following the American surrender at Detroit, public pressure grew to have the other US forces on the Canadian border advance. Many felt that the Detroit debacle was a disgrace to America that must be avenged as soon as possible. To politicians, journalists, and citizens alike, the Niagara border appeared to be the place where an invasion could easily be accomplished and the shame of Detroit's surrender avenged.

This was the era of warfare in which the smoothbore musket was the primary infantry weapon, requiring opposing forces to be capable of maneuvering and fighting at close range. In June 1812 the British Army was one of the world's best armies, if not the best. In contrast, the US Army was a collection of amateurs. Two years later, however, US regulars could stand their ground and fight their British opponents to a draw. This book compares and contrasts US regular infantry and British regular infantry during the War of 1812 in the Canadian theater. It features regiments of both countries that fought on the Niagara border in 1812 and 1814 and during the 1813 St. Lawrence expedition.

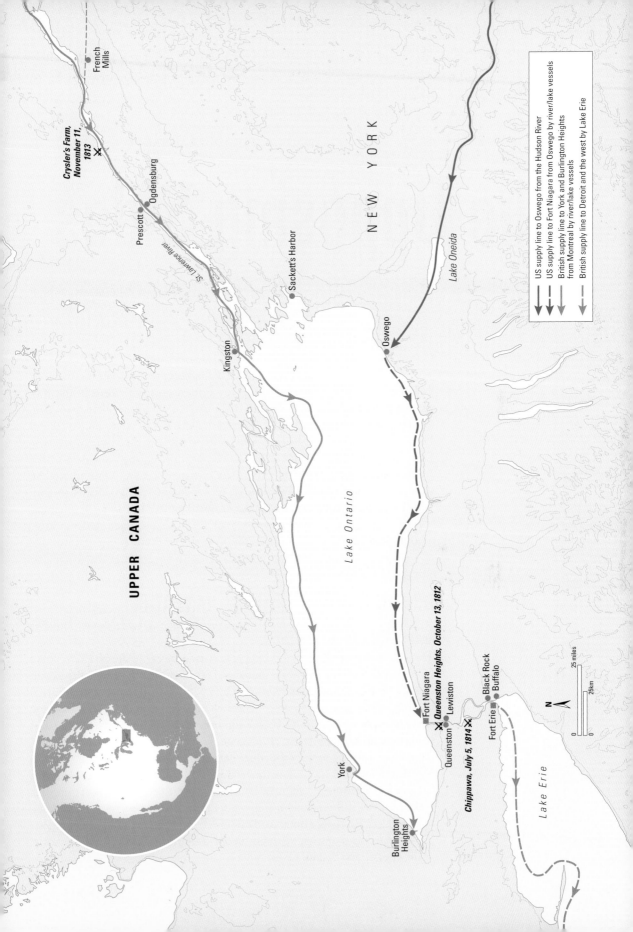

UPPER CANADA

NEW YORK

Lake Ontario

Lake Erie

Lake Oneida

St Lawrence River

French Mills

Crysler's Farm, November 11, 1813

Ogdensburg

Prescott

Sackett's Harbor

Kingston

Oswego

York

Burlington Heights

Fort Niagara

Queenston Heights, October 13, 1812

Queenston

Lewiston

Black Rock

Buffalo

Fort Erie

Chippawa, July 5, 1814

US supply line to Oswego from the Hudson River
US supply line to Fort Niagara from Oswego by river/lake vessels
British supply line to York and Burlington Heights from Montreal by river/lake vessels
British supply line to Detroit and the west by Lake Erie

N

0 25 miles

0 25 km

The Opposing Sides

Logistics, finance, geography, and – for Britain – the demands of the war against Napoleonic France restricted the size of the forces that fought in Canada during the War of 1812. The battles of this war were comparable to European divisional and brigade actions. For example, the battle of Lundy's Lane (July 25, 1814) beside the Niagara River involved approximately 2,500 American and 3,500 British troops. In comparison, the battle of Maida (July 4, 1806) in southern Italy involved approximately 5,000 French and 5,000 British troops; and the Duke of Wellington's victory at Salamanca (July 22, 1812) pitted approximately 51,000 British and allied troops against 49,000 French.

ORIGINS, ORGANIZATION, LINEAGE

American

The US Army of the War of 1812 came into being in April 1785 when Congress authorized the recruitment of 700 men directly into government service. The size and composition of the US Army fluctuated as frontier warfare waxed and waned and a crisis with Revolutionary France led to a series of small naval actions. By the summer of 1800 the Regular Army was composed of four regiments of infantry, two regiments of artillery, and two companies of dragoons. Reductions left the US Army with two infantry regiments and one artillery regiment by 1807, but international concerns led to an expansion in 1808. By 1811 there were seven infantry regiments (1st–7th), one rifle regiment, one regiment of artillerists, one regiment of light artillery (in theory horse artillery), and one regiment of light dragoons.

Increased tensions with Britain caused Congress to expand the US Army again in early 1812, adding ten more infantry regiments, two more artillery

"Heroes of '76." American Revolutionary War militia mythology, exemplified in this print, contributed to US failure at Queenston Heights. In reality, the Revolutionary militia had been mainly a guerrilla and internal-security force. Fighting the British Army in open battle successfully had required the regulars of George Washington's Continental Army. (Library of Congress, LC-DIG-pga-09082)

regiments, and a second dragoon regiment. After war with Britain was declared on June 18, 1812, eight more infantry regiments were added. On paper this was a force of over 35,000 men. Fewer than 7,000 personnel were enrolled, however, mostly in the 11 regiments raised prior to 1812, and were spread across the frontier in small detachments. After fighting started and the militia units failed to live up to expectations, more regular units were created. In 1813 Congress authorized 20 more infantry regiments, of which 19 were raised. In 1814 four more infantry regiments and three rifle regiments were added, the dragoons were consolidated into one regiment, and the artillery regiments were reorganized into an Artillery Corps of 48 companies and the Light Artillery Regiment. By the end of the war in February 1815, during which time some regiments were consolidated, the US Army had 44 infantry regiments and four rifle regiments in service.

American infantry regiments initially had several different organizations. The 1st and 2d Infantry were authorized an aggregate strength of 806, while the 3d through 7th were authorized 849. Regimental strengths actually varied from 302 to 577. The ten new infantry regiments raised in 1812 were each to consist of two 1,000-man battalions. On June 26, 1812, Congress mandated a single regimental organization based on ten companies with a strength of roughly 1,000 men. During the war, however, most regiments were less than half this size.

The Light Artillery Regiment had ten companies and the three artillery regiments had 20 companies each. These companies were distributed across the country as needed, but only a few were used as field artillery. A field-artillery company would generally man three guns (two cannons and a howitzer, or three cannons) as a half-battery. Most artillery companies manned fortifications or served as infantry – the 3d Artillery became known as one of the best "infantry" units in the US Army. In early 1814 Congress ordered consolidation of the three artillery regiments into an Artillery Corps, reducing the number of companies to 48. The Light Artillery was not part of this consolidation.

This private of the 11th Infantry is ready for combat. He is holding his musket in the firing position and has left his pack and bedroll in the regiment's camp before moving to the battlefield.

Weapons, dress, and equipment

The soldier's musket (**1**) is the US M1795, 60in in length with a barrel bore of .69in.

He wears a shako (**2**) of the Belgic type adopted in 1813, referred to as a "tombstone" shako because of the slight vertical extension of the top front, and an 1814-pattern shako plate (**3**). His gray "roundabout" jacket (**4**) is in the style that was issued to Scott's 1st Brigade. The supply system could not provide the regulation blue and Scott insisted that all regiments in his brigade were uniformly clothed. His white canvas trousers (**5**) are grubby but in good shape,

having been issued just weeks before. On his feet he wears leather buckle shoes (**6**) that were wearable on either foot.

The black leather belts (**7**) crossing his chest support the black leather cartridge box (**8**) and bayonet scabbard (**9**). The steel bayonet is 1in wide at the base, 18in long, and has a triangular cross section that narrows to a sharp pointed end. In the center of his belts is a plain oval belt plate made of brass. He wears a linen haversack (**10**) used to store rations on the march. Painted light blue, his wooden canteen (**11**) is suspended on a strap over his right shoulder.

Prewar US Army regiments were scattered from Maine to Louisiana in detachments of one or several companies. New regiments frequently had newly organized companies detached and sent to the crises of the day. In a reported order of battle it was common for a listed "regiment" to be composed of companies from itself and other regiments (what the British termed a "battalion of detachments"), regimental designation corresponding to the senior officer present or the regiment having the most companies present. This ad hoc organization eroded unit cohesion, however, as men and companies would serve under unfamiliar commanders.

Later in the war several militia-based volunteer units proved successful as auxiliaries to regulars. For decades the United States had relied for defense on the states' militias, which were organized into regionally based regiments. The Uniform Militia Act of 1792 was intended to create a ready militia that should have encompassed all able-bodied men, but muster rolls were not up to date, training was inadequate (if it even existed at all), and weapons were frequently in poor condition. Western states such as Kentucky and Tennessee, being frequently in conflict with Indian populations, had kept their militias in better condition than the older states. Militiamen proved no match for British regulars in open combat, though they sometimes succeeded in defending again British regulars when placed in field fortifications. The western states' militias performed effectively against Indians in the Northwest, West, and South. Successful use of militias required senior leadership that understood their strengths and weaknesses and did not expect these units to perform like regulars.

British

The British Army originated as three separate armies in the late 1600s. These were the English, Scottish, and Irish establishments funded by the three respective parliaments. The English and Scottish establishments were amalgamated in 1707 into the British Army, but the Irish establishment remained separate until 1800.

The Army expanded in wartime by raising new regiments or adding battalions to existing regiments. When peace came, regiments would be disbanded and the Army shrank. Examples of the number of infantry regiments in service before 1815 are: 1793 (start of the French Revolution), 81 regiments; 1794, 135 regiments (on paper); 1812, 104 regiments. Regiments were numbered according to seniority. During reductions, regiments were retained based on their seniority.

Outside the British Army's seniority sequence there were local regiments known as "fencibles" or "provincials." Fencibles were raised in their province to serve within it. In the case of Canada, fencibles could not be sent outside of Canada's borders. Fencible volunteers had no prospect of being sent to the Caribbean, Europe, or the East Indies, and this helped recruitment. Fencible regiments raised in Canada were trained to the standard of the regulars and performed as well as their British Army cousins on the battlefield.

British regiments, unlike American, could have one or multiple battalions. In 1814 there were 27 regiments with a single battalion, 71 with two battalions,

four with three battalions, and two with four or more battalions. A regiment's battalions seldom if ever served together. A battalion was composed of ten companies: two flank companies (one grenadier and one light) and eight center companies. Authorized size for a battalion depended on where it was stationed: there were lower numbers for home service and higher numbers for overseas garrisons and battalions fighting the French in Europe. Prewar regiments in Canada appear to have been authorized 600 or 800 corporals and privates. Actual numbers were less due to peacetime attrition, detached personnel, and absences.

British artillery forces in Canada were from the Royal Regiment of Artillery, also referred to as the Royal Artillery (RA). There were ten RA battalions, each with ten companies. The companies were deployed without regard to their battalion, which served as an administrative entity. An RA company could serve as a field-artillery battery (called a brigade in this period) serving five field guns and one howitzer. Alternatively, a company could man heavy guns in fortifications or siege batteries. British artillery companies never served as substitute infantry like the Americans.

In June 1812 there were seven British infantry battalions in Canada: four regular, one garrison, and two fencible. With four artillery companies this amounted to about 6,000 men scattered in company and multi-company posts. In Nova Scotia, New Brunswick, and Prince Edward Island there were one fencible and four regular battalions with five artillery companies, roughly 3,700 men.

Canada had a regionally based militia. Under the direction of British regulars, Canadian militia regiments had their best men formed into a pair of flank companies. These companies trained more intensely than the rest of the militia regiment (and more than any American militia unit) and were equipped as well as the British supply situation allowed. They proved their worth and in 1813 a battalion was formed from selected flank companies. This was designated the Volunteer Incorporated Militia Battalion and became equivalent to a regular unit in terms of training, discipline, and performance.

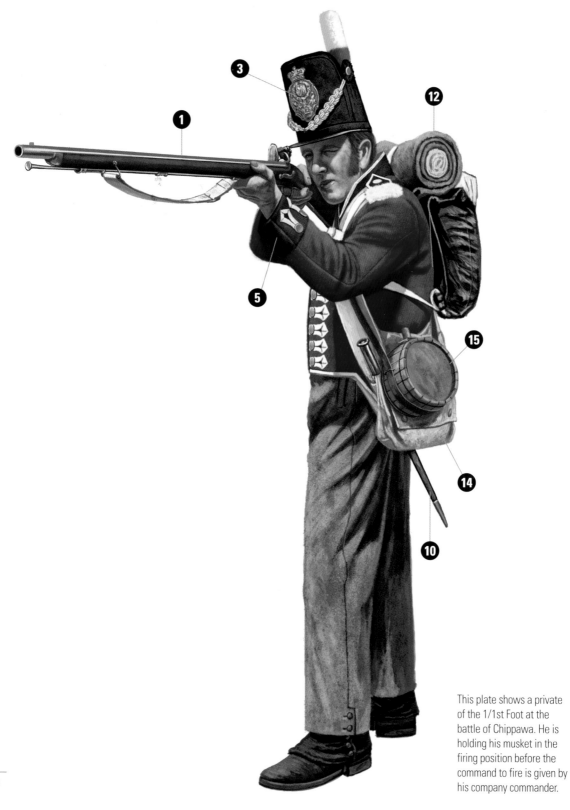

This plate shows a private of the 1/1st Foot at the battle of Chippawa. He is holding his musket in the firing position before the command to fire is given by his company commander.

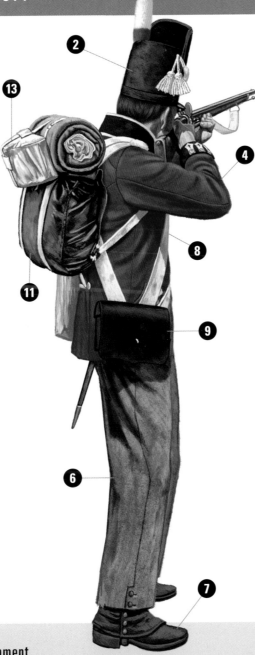

Weapons, dress, and equipment

This soldier is armed with an India Pattern Musket (**1**), also known as the "Brown Bess." The musket is 54.33in long with a bore of .75in.

He wears an 1812-pattern shako (**2**) made of wool felt. It is approximately 8¼in high at the front with a black leather peak; on the front is a brass plate (**3**) and on the left side a black rosette with a regimental button in front of the worsted plume. The plume colors indicate a center company. He wears the distinctive red coat (**4**) of the British soldier. The 1/1st Foot's regimental facing color was royal blue (**5**). His drop-front trousers (**6**) are made of gray wool. He wears low buckle shoes (**7**) made of leather that were wearable on either foot. Soldiers alternated shoes on each foot to give better wear.

White leather belts (**8**) cross his chest, supporting the cartridge box (**9**) and bayonet scabbard (**10**). The steel bayonet is 18in long and 1in wide at the base and has a triangular cross section that narrows to a sharp pointed end. The regimental belt plate is specific to the regiment in which the soldier served. He wears a backpack (**11**) with a rolled blanket (**12**) and a mess tin (**13**) strapped to it. On the rear of his left hip is a linen haversack (**14**), used to carry rations on the march. Made of wood and lined with beeswax, his blue-painted canteen (**15**) is suspended from a strap over his right shoulder.

LEADERSHIP AND RECRUITMENT

American

When compared with the British Army, the US Army was an amateur force, as was clearly revealed by examining the officer corps. The prewar Regular Army was scattered in small detachments and officers typically dealt with company drill and frontier skirmishing. The majority of new regimental and company officers commissioned from civilian life owed their position to political connections or nepotism. New regiments lacked experienced cadres, although an effort was made to provide some experienced officers and men from prewar regulars. One of the greatest deficiencies may have been the lack of experienced non-commissioned officers to teach and oversee training, drill, and combat.

Beyond company-level functions, a US Army officer's professional knowledge was dependent upon an individual's own studies. Some officers

Pictured here in 1809, Alexander Macomb was born in Detroit in 1782 and went on to become one of the outstanding American officers in the War of 1812. Promoted to brigadier general in January 1814, he commanded troops opposing the British Lake Champlain offensive. Macomb was Commanding General of the US Army from 1828 to his death in 1841. (Library of Congress, LC-DIG-pga-13346)

Major General Andrew Jackson was a Tennessee politician and prewar militia general. During the war he was commissioned in the US Army and led the campaign in the south which culminated with his victory at the battle of New Orleans. He remained in the US Army until 1821 when he returned to politics. Elected president in 1828, he served two terms. His Indian Removal Act forced most of the Cherokee, Choctaw, Creek, Chickasaw, and Seminole peoples to uproot their lives and move to what is now Oklahoma state. (Stock Montage/Stock Montage/Getty Images)

made use of various European texts to learn about their profession beyond company drill and skirmishing. These self-educated officers provided the men who became successful leaders. One such regular was Winfield Scott, who acquired and studied his own library of military texts. Scott later described the regular officer corps in caustic terms. He wrote that the pre-1808 officer corps was "generally sunk into either sloth, ignorance, or habits of intemperate drinking," while his fellow officers appointed in 1808 (when Scott was commissioned captain in the Light Artillery) were "coarse and ignorant men … which always turned out utterly unfit for any military purpose whatever"; he added, "The officers appointed to the large augmentations of the army in 1812 and 1813, by President Madison, were, from nearly the same reasons, of the same general character" (Scott 1864: 35). Few officers had the knowledge needed properly to command and administer forces in the field. For officers and men, actual war would be their schooling.

Dating from 1804, this illustration depicts Brigadier General William H. Winder, the defeated American commander at the battle of Bladensburg on August 24, 1814. Winder's defeat at the hands of Major-General Robert Ross resulted in the capture and burning of Washington. (Library of Congress, LC-DIG-pga-13378)

Recruitment for the Regular Army was difficult during the War of 1812 and units remained chronically understrength. Most men preferred to serve in their state and territorial militias instead of with the regulars; this would keep them closer to home and allow shorter terms of service. US Army service was not highly regarded at this time, resulting in recruits being drawn from the economically disadvantaged. Despite a cash bounty paid upon enlistment, a bonus of three months' pay, and a land grant of 160 acres upon the end of an enlistment, men were always in short supply. Recruiting was haphazard at the start of the war. Officers would attempt to raise men while not knowing to which regiment they were assigned. When 100 men were assembled the group would move to a training camp and a company would be formed. In August 1812, confusion caused by this method led to assigning each regiment a geographic recruiting region and placing its colonel in charge. A colonel would task officers with recruiting and assign others to command companies. Infantry regiments recruited within one or two states. The new artillery regiments recruited from multi-state regions; the 2d Artillery recruited in Maryland and states south while the 3d Artillery recruited north of Maryland.

British

Two-thirds of the British Army's infantry officers were the product of the purchase system in which one paid to buy a commission. The remaining one-third were a mix of men who had initially purchased a junior commission and were subsequently promoted for their service and those who were commissioned from the enlisted and NCO ranks, usually for heroism in action. Although former enlisted men were seldom promoted beyond junior officer ranks, these men provided a cadre of experienced combat officers. As the worldwide war against Napoleon continued, combat, overseas deployments, and sickness weeded out dilettantes and incompetents, causing the number of officers with non-purchased commissions to rise in battalions stationed overseas.

Company-level officers were generally competent. Reforms directed by the British Army's Commander-in-Chief, the Duke of York (served 1795–1809 and 1811–27), had improved the officer corps and the treatment of enlisted men. Regulations were introduced aimed at preventing the purchase of

IXᵀᴴ ᴏʀ E. NORFOLK REGIMENT ᴏꜰ INFANTRY.

OPPOSITE
The eight battalion companies of a British regiment of foot in echelon as derived from the British manual. The echelon allowed a British regiment to maneuver with far greater ease than a rigid line. Individual companies could move as needed without rigid adherence to their neighboring companies. (Drawing by author)

commissions as captains and majors by young, inexperienced men. Efforts were made to prevent incompetents from being promoted and requiring officers to demonstrate that they knew their jobs. Officers were expected to concern themselves with the state of their men and ensure that their units were trained and ready when called to action. The Duke of York's reforms built the army that the Duke of Wellington led to victory in Portugal and Spain, and the army that fought in North America.

British enlisted men originally signed up for life, but the wartime need for more men led to the creation of a seven-year enlistment term during the Napoleonic Wars. Those who joined were mostly landless poor, jobless laborers in need of money, or criminals. Although there was no conscription, men legally classed as vagrants could be forced to enlist. Service was not considered desirable by the rest of the population and soldiers were looked down upon. Despite many being society's outcasts, hard discipline and rigorous training turned these men into the world's best infantry by 1812.

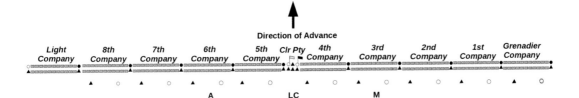

WEAPONS AND TACTICS

The standard infantry weapon was the smoothbore musket to which a bayonet could be attached. Muskets were muzzle-loading and fired spherical lead balls. Musket barrels were not rifled and the balls were of a smaller diameter than the barrel. This made loading faster, but still required a choreographed sequence of steps to load black powder (the propellant), ball, and wadding (to keep the ball in the barrel and tight against the powder). The powder and ball would be contained in a premeasured paper cartridge. A soldier would tear or bite the end of the cartridge, pour a small amount of the powder into the primer pan, then the rest of the powder down the barrel, drop in the ball, then place the paper in the muzzle. He then used his ramrod vigorously to tamp the paper, ball, and powder into a compact mass. The priming powder would be ignited by sparks created by a flint striking hard steel. Once successfully loaded and fired, the ball would travel down the barrel, literally bouncing off the sides as it moved, until it exited with an erratic trajectory.

Aimed fire was difficult beyond a few dozen yards and then only by the best-trained and most experienced soldiers or hunters. Infantry used volley fire in combat and could inflict heavy losses on a formed body of enemy troops. Musket volleys created large clouds of grayish-white smoke. Repeated volleys, in the absence of a good breeze, would leave the infantry lines wreathed in smoke and unable to see each other. This added to soldiers' fears because they could not see whether the enemy was advancing upon them.

This image is derived from *Rules and Regulations for the Formation, Field-Exercise, and Movements, of His Majesty's Forces* and shows the two-rank firing line. The color guard is in the center of the companies. The letters "LC," "M," and "A" denote the positions of the lieutenant-colonel, major, and adjutant respectively. The captain of each company is in the first rank of the rightmost file; behind him is the senior sergeant. The leftmost company has a junior officer followed by a sergeant (or corporal) in the left file. These men are in a third "skeleton" rank in the other nine companies. (Drawing by author)

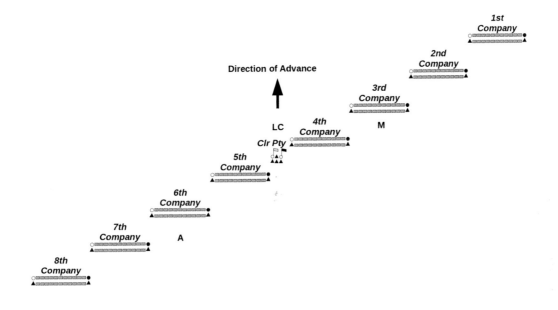

The standard US flintlock musket was the .69-caliber M1795, based on the French M1763 or "Charleville" musket. Produced in Federal arsenals and by contractors, the M1795 weighed 10lb, was 60in long and had a barrel length of 42in. Rate of fire was two to three rounds per minute. (NRA Museums, NRAmuseums.com)

Musket misfires were common in combat. These could be caused by broken or improperly aligned flints, the primer powder being damp or loose, the primer hole being blocked by ash from prior firing, or bad black powder in the barrel. In combat a soldier who had a misfire would have to take time to fix the problem – assuming he recognized it and remembered in the heat of action how to remedy it. Some soldiers, especially new recruits, could fail to notice a misfire and continue to load and try to fire. Muskets have been recovered from battlefields and found to contain loaded multiple loads of powder and ball. An overloaded musket could explode, injuring or killing the soldier and those nearby.

Bayonets were attached to muskets, especially by the British. These were sharpened steel blades up to 16in long with a triangular cross section. Bayonets could be deadly in close combat, but more often their use served a psychological purpose. New and inexperienced troops, such as the Americans in 1812 and 1813, would frequently refuse to charge their opponents with fixed bayonets or flee from an opposing line charging with fixed bayonets. Well-trained soldiers with high morale would charge with fixed bayonets against a despised or disorganized opponent, however. Bayonet charges seldom resulted in actual hand-to-hand melees; either the defenders fled or the attackers stopped short and began a close-range firefight.

The British Army used the India Pattern Musket (originally adopted by the East India Company for its indigenous soldiers), commonly known as the

"Brown Bess." This had a .75 bore (a barrel diameter of .75in) that was well constructed and as reliable as a flintlock could be. The Brown Bess had the lowest misfire rate of any musket of the time and was highly regarded by the Americans, who had purchased 11,000 before the war.

The most numerous type of musket used by the Americans was the US-made M1795. This had a .69 bore and was based on the Revolutionary War-era French M1763 "light musket," also known as the "Charleville" musket. Two government facilities, in Springfield, Massachusetts, and Harper's Ferry, Virginia, produced over 150,000 M1795 muskets between 1795 and 1815. Thousands more were manufactured by private contractors. The M1795 would go on to be used through the American Civil War (1861–65), many having been converted from flintlock to percussion ignition.

American riflemen used the M1803 rifle, made at the Harper's Ferry Federal Arsenal, or the M1807 rifle produced by private contractors. These were .54-bore muzzle-loading rifles and were very accurate in the hands of a well-trained soldier. The rifle ball fit tightly in the barrel and had to be rammed home against the rifling. A rifle took longer to load than a smoothbore – it required fine priming powder in addition to the regular coarser gunpowder used to propel the ball – but could be accurately fired at ranges up to 300yd. There were no British rifle-equipped units in Canada.

Both sides used limited amounts of field artillery during the war. Like muskets, the artillery guns of this period were muzzle-loading and smoothbore

The British and Canadians used the legendary "Brown Bess" musket, officially the India Pattern Musket. It had a .75in bore, weighed 9.68lb, had a barrel length of 39in, and an overall length of 55.25in. Rate of fire was three to six rounds per minute. (© Royal Armouries XII.5537)

| 8th Company | 7th Company | 6th Company | 5th Company | Color Guard | Direction of Advance | 4th Company | 3rd Company | 2nd Company | 1st Company | 2nd Elite Company | 1st Elite Company |

SM

A

M

LC

C

US manuals used the three-rank French line. This drawing, based on Smyth's *Regulations for the Field Exercise, Manœuvres, and Conduct of the Infantry of the United States*, shows a theoretical ten-company regiment deployed in line. Captains are in the first rank, with a sergeant in the third rank behind them. The fourth rank comprised (left to right): a sergeant, the ensign, the first lieutenant, two sergeants, and the second lieutenant. The left company has a sergeant and a senior corporal on its left flank. This regiment includes a colonel ("C"), a lieutenant colonel ("LC"), a major ("M"), and an adjutant ("A"). (Drawing by author)

weapons. Rate of fire was one round or less per minute, and the heavier the gun the slower the rate. The most common field piece was a 6pdr cannon, so named for firing a 3.5in-diameter iron ball weighing approximately 6lb. The 6pdr's theoretical range was 1,000yd for a ball (round shot); effective range was less. In addition to round shot, both sides used canister shot. Essentially, canister shot was a lightweight cylinder filled with musket balls. When fired, the cylinder broke apart and the balls spread out like a shotgun blast. Canister rounds were used against approaching infantry at close range (less than 600yd).

In several battles the Americans brought heavier 12pdr and 18pdr cannons to the field, but these were less mobile and frequently did not see action. The British used a pair of 24pdr cannons along the Niagara frontier in 1814. Howitzers firing explosive shells were part of the field artillery. On paper, 5.5in howitzers comprised one-sixth of a British RA brigade and one-third of a US artillery company. The 5.5in howitzer threw shells to a maximum range of 1,000yd, but was usually used at ranges of half that. British howitzers could fire the recently invented shrapnel shell, but these were in short supply in Canada during the wars against Napoleon and rarely used until the second half of 1814.

A War of 1812 battle was dominated by infantry, therefore the infantry drill and tactics were critical. British forces started the war with the distinct advantage of having a well-disciplined, well-trained, and cohesive force, even if it was small. British doctrine was based on one standard manual: *Rules and Regulations for the Formation, Field-Exercise, and Movements, of His Majesty's Forces*, originally issued June 1, 1792 (updates had been made by General Orders in 1803, 1804, and 1809). This manual provided the British Army with a uniform repertoire of formations, movements, actions, and

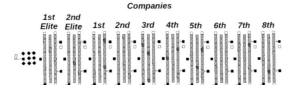

Companies

1st Elite 2nd Elite 1st 2nd 3rd 4th 5th 6th 7th 8th

the necessary commands to execute them, based on the British preference for linear fighting that maximized the effectiveness of smoothbore muskets on a battlefield. Any British soldier and battalion would understand these commands, even if they were new to a larger formation.

In contrast, the US Army was the victim of doctrinal indecision and political machinations, leading to three separate manuals. The first and oldest manual was the Revolutionary War-era *Regulations for the Order and Discipline of the Troops of the United States* (known as the "Blue Book") by Baron von Steuben. This was based on mid-18th-century European doctrine which Steuben simplified for the nonprofessional, less extensively trained, American Army and militias. In early 1812 the US War Department ordered the regular infantry to adopt a manual by Alexander Smyth, *Regulations for the Field Exercise, Manœuvres, and Conduct of the Infantry of the United States*, which was an abridgment of the 1791 French infantry regulations for battlefield doctrine and Steuben's rules for camps. After Smyth failed as a general officer in the 1812 campaign and was removed from the US Army, the War Department ordered the use of a third manual, *A Hand Book for Infantry*, by William Duane. Like Smyth, Duane borrowed from the 1791 French manual and Steuben. Unfortunately, Duane's manual was no improvement over that of Smyth. The result was that officers in the field used whichever of the three manuals they wished, in whole or in part. It was left to local senior officers to select drill and doctrine for their commands.

Battles started with enemies facing one another in lines of battle. Whoever chose the field of battle was likely either defending, or starting off in a defensive position. Whenever possible a force sought a position on higher ground with secure flanks. A secure flank could be provided by a river, swamp,

or other difficult or impassable terrain. Lines formed up facing each other, beyond musket and artillery range whenever possible. It was up to the attacker to close the distance and bring his forces into the range of the defending force's weapons. Artillery was not capable of overhead fire, so it would either be placed on the flanks of an advancing infantry line to shell the defenders, or at a critical spot in the defense to blast an advancing enemy with canister. American forces frequently used a three-rank formation (as their French-based doctrine called for) while the British used their traditional two-rank line. Later in the war the American regulars started to use a two-rank line as well, once training and experience had demonstrated its superiority in firefights.

Once the lines closed to about 100yd, the infantry volleys would begin. In this firefight the rate of fire was more important than marksmanship. These volleys were intended to disrupt the opposing infantry, cause loss of cohesion, and reduce morale in preparation for a bayonet charge. When the enemy appeared to be wavering, the order to charge would be given. Once the charge began, the defenders either broke and fled, or the attackers would hesitate and stop to resume firing. Seldom did troops actually engage in bayonet fighting. Throughout 1812 and 1813 American units would usually break at the sight of an advancing line of British bayonets. By the 1814 campaign, however, both sides' regulars would stand and fight a musket duel at point-blank range.

LOGISTICS

Both sides found supplying their armies in the field to be a major problem. Roads were limited and in poor conditions. Contractors were relied upon to provided wagons and animals, but these civilians were frequently unwilling to work close to the fighting fronts and were not required to cross international boundaries. Water transport was cheaper and more efficient, but geography placed obstacles in the way of both sides' supply boats in the form of waterfalls, rapids, and watersheds between rivers. All of these obstacles necessitated the use of land transport to move supplies around them, thus compounding the shortfall in land transport.

The prewar US supply system was inadequate to support a wartime force. The US Army did not have a Quartermaster Department until Congress created one in 1812 along with a Purchasing Department, authorizing a quartermaster officer for each regiment who reported to the regimental commander. Quartermaster officers (usually general officers) were appointed to command above regimental level and they reported to both their immediate superior and to the Quartermaster General in Washington, DC. Parallel to the Quartermaster Department was the Purchasing Department, responsible for procurement and delivering supplies to the Quartermaster Department, which then had to move material and supplies to the field. Each department reported directly to the Secretary of War.

Americans moved supplies from their major depots (for the Niagara and Lake Champlain fronts this was mainly New York) to the river landing closest to the next transport line. Cargo would then be carried across watersheds to the next river (or lake) and then reloaded on small craft and moved to the next depot. This process would be repeated as often as needed until supplies

reached the troops at the front. The supply system was run by inexperienced officials, some of whom were corrupt, causing heavy wastage (and theft) and resulting in unreliable delivery. Keeping troops fed and supplied with ammunition was a constant struggle for American commanders and staffs.

British supply started in Britain. Practically everything needed had to be shipped across the Atlantic Ocean to Canada. Because the St. Lawrence River was navigable by ocean transports to Montreal, it was easy to get supplies to Canada – as long as the transports were not intercepted by the US Navy or American privateers. Then the problem became similar to that experienced by the US supply system: supplies had to be carried around waterfalls and rapids, and then moved to the front. The use of Lake Ontario as a supply line was constrained by the naval contest for control of the lake. Transports that sailed alone were vulnerable to interception by enemy ships, but waiting for convoys to assemble and sail under escort slowed delivery. The frontier character of the battlefront meant that local transportation resources were limited once one left the lakes and rivers, and wagons and draft animals had to be imported. As with the Americans, British supply was always a critical consideration in planning.

The British had a distinct advantage in logistics: their 20-odd years of near-continuous experience during the French Revolutionary Wars (1792–1802) and the Napoleonic Wars (1803–15). Managing supply for forces around the globe, ranging from peacetime Canada through wars in Portugal, Sicily, Egypt, India, South America, and South Africa, had given British logicians unmatched experience. While forces in Canada fought with limited supplies, these resources were allocated based on balancing the needs of global requirements. Once peace returned to Europe in mid-1814, however, the war against the United States took precedence for supply.

These American soldiers of 1812 are shown wearing unrealistically neat and tidy uniforms. Perhaps one of the great public misconceptions about uniforms is that soldiers in the field were neatly dressed. In reality, their uniforms quickly became ragged, patched, and dirty. (Kean Collection/Getty Images)

Queenston Heights

October 13, 1812

BACKGROUND TO BATTLE

This illustration, published in 1814, shows Fort Niagara as viewed from the British side of the river at Newark. (Library of Congress, LC-USZ62-53568)

The US commander on the Niagara front was Major General Stephen Van Rensselaer, whose only military experience to date had been in the peacetime militia. To compensate for his lack of experience, Van Rensselaer appointed his nephew Solomon Van Rensselaer, a former major of regulars (served 1792–1800), as his aide. The Niagara command soon fell into disarray when

recently promoted Brigadier General Alexander Smyth arrived at Black Rock, New York, with a brigade of newly recruited regulars. Being a regular, but with only four years' service, Smyth believed he should be in command and refused to meet personally with the militia general. This friction would result in Smyth's Brigade, containing half of the regulars on the Niagara front, staying in camp during the impending fight.

By October Van Rensselaer's army had around 2,500 regulars and 4,000 militiamen. Most were newly recruited, inadequately trained, ill-equipped, and experiencing a variety of illnesses that diminished the number of men available for duty. These men wanted to take the war into Canada. Politically, pressure mounted from all directions for an attack on the Niagara border. Van Rensselaer saw the need for action and on September 17 wrote: "A retrograde movement of this army upon the back of that disaster which has befallen the one at Detroit, would stamp a stigma upon the national character which time could never wipe away" (quoted in Van Rensselaer 1836: 17). His superior, Major General Henry Dearborn, told him in a September 26 letter: "At all events, we must calculate on possessing Upper Canada before winter sets in" (quoted in Van Rensselaer 1836: Appx 60). Van Rensselaer decided to attack across the Niagara using a mixed force of militiamen and regulars on the night of October 10–11. The attack would cross the river between Lewiston, New York and the village of Queenston, Ontario, north of the Niagara Falls.

On the Canadian side of the river, the chain of command was clear. All troops, regular and militia, were firmly under command of Major-General Isaac Brock. An aggressive officer, who had forced the surrender in August of the American forces at Detroit, Brock was under orders not to take the offensive along the Niagara. While Brock commanded all of Upper Canada, Major-General Roger Sheaffe commanded the Niagara border. By October,

ABOVE LEFT
Major-General Isaac Brock was governor and commander of Upper Canada at the start of the War of 1812. He became a British and Canadian hero when he captured the American Northwest Army at Detroit, Michigan, in August 1812. Brock was a solidly professional officer who believed in acting decisively – a trait that would cost him his life. (Hulton Archive/Getty Images)

ABOVE RIGHT
James Wilkinson, pictured here in 1798, was one of two American brigadier generals at the start of the War of 1812. Earlier he was a paid Spanish spy. His military incompetence and political machinations were the cause of several American defeats. It was said that he never won a battle, but never lost a court martial. (Fotosearch/Getty Images)

A view of the Niagara River from Queenston Heights, Canada, looking north toward Lake Ontario. This engraving shows the Heights' commanding view of both the Canadian and American sides of the river. Without control of the Heights, an army's movements would be known to an enemy on the top. Capturing the Heights was the only objective identified by the American commander, Major General Van Rensselaer, for his attack on October 13, 1812. (Universal History Archive/ Universal Images Group via Getty Images)

Brock had collected elements of the 1/41st and 1/49th Foot, two flank companies of the Royal Newfoundland Fencibles, one RA company, local militiamen, and some 300 Indian allies for a total force of 2,340 officers and men (1,230 regulars). These were deployed in four main groupings along the Niagara, being (from north to south): at and near Fort George (1,005 men); Queenston (420); Chippawa (436); and Fort Erie (476). Artillery pieces were placed in fortifications, prepared positions, and two mobile half-batteries (one RA and one militia). British regulars were greatly superior to the Americans in training, experience, and discipline. Well aware of the situation in his enemy's camps, Brock believed that defeating another American force, as he had at Detroit, would have a far-reaching impact on the war. Brock eschewed a passive defense, therefore any American crossing of the Niagara would be counterattacked.

The question facing Brock concerned where the Americans would attack. At the north end of the Niagara, the British held Fort George where the Niagara flowed into Lake Ontario. At the southern end, where Lake Erie flowed into the Niagara, was Fort Erie. The falls were about halfway along the river, which in the vicinity of the falls was too fast and turbulent for an attack. The British therefore expected that possible American attacks would be in the south from Black Rock and Buffalo, New York, directed against the Fort Erie region, or in the north from Fort Niagara and Youngstown, New York, against Fort George. The presence of Smyth's Brigade of American regulars at Black Rock led Brock to consider an attack against Fort Erie was likely.

The first American attempt to cross the Niagara failed to get underway due to a storm and a lack of oars for the boats to be used. The operation's

cancellation meant that Major General Van Rensselaer now felt even more political pressure to attack:

> … the previously excited ardor [of the soldiers] seemed to have gained new heat from the late miscarriage; the brave were mortified to stop short of their object, and the timid thought laurels half won by the attempt.
>
> On the morning of the 12th, such was the pressure upon me from all quarters, that I became satisfied that my refusal to act might involve me in suspicion, and the service in disgrace. (Quoted in Van Rensselaer 1836: 64)

The river crossing was now planned for early morning October 13. The planning was simplistic; no objectives were identified other than crossing the river and capturing Queenston Heights (commonly referred to as "the Heights") and the village. With only 13 boats available, the force would take some considerable time to cross. The attackers comprised miscellaneous regular detachments and the New York State Militia. The initial crossing was planned in three waves under the command of Colonel Solomon Van Rensselaer. The first wave included 40 regular artillerymen, 150 regulars (13th Infantry), and 150 militiamen; the second wave was composed of regulars from the 13th Infantry and a detachment from Fort Niagara; and the third wave was made up of the remaining regulars. After the third wave, the rest of the militiamen would cross into Canada. Artillery support was provided by two 18pdr cannons in Fort Gray atop Lewis Heights, an unidentified mortar located near the fort, and two 6pdr field guns located at Lewiston.

A watercolor of Queenston village painted by Edward Walsh, surgeon of the 1/49th Foot stationed in Canada 1803–07. The wooded Queenston Heights rises with the dirt Portage Road climbing the hillside. The Niagara River, gorge, and the high ground on the American side of the river are clearly shown. (Library of Congress, LCCN 2004662211)

1 Early morning: British initial forces deploy at Queenston village and on Queenston Heights.

2 c.0400hrs: US troops, led by a detachment of regulars, embark near Lewiston, New York. Troops of the New York State Militia follow in subsequent crossings.

3 c.0430–0500hrs: After landing below the Heights, Captain John Wool (13th Infantry) leads an attack toward Queenston.

4 c.0500hrs: The 1/49th Foot's grenadier company halts Wool's advance.

5 c.0530hrs: Wool retreats to the landing site.

6 c.0530hrs: After shooting at the US troops landing below them, the 1/49th Foot's light company is withdrawn from the Heights to help defend Queenston.

7 c.0600hrs: Wool leads his troops along the riverbank to a location where his men can scale the Heights.

8 c.0630hrs: Finding the Heights unoccupied, Wool swiftly captures the redan and deploys to hold his position.

9 c.0700–0730hrs: Major-General Isaac Brock, having arrived from Fort George, gathers up a small force of men from the 1/49th Foot's light company and local militia, and attacks the Americans now holding the Heights. The attack fails and Brock is killed.

10 c.0800–0900hrs: More US troops cross the Niagara and join Wool on the Heights.

11 c.0800–0900hrs: British skirmishers (the 1/49th Foot's light company and local militia) probe the US troops from the west woods. After the light company's commander, Captain John Williams, is wounded they retreat to Queenston.

12 c.1100–1430hrs: Lieutenant Colonel Winfield Scott arrives on the Heights and takes command. His troops skirmish with Canadian militiamen and Indians in woods west of their position.

13 c.1300–1430hrs: Major-General Robert Sheaffe arrives at Queenston and decides to march his force west and around the Americans in order to be able to attack on top of the Niagara Escarpment from the south.

14 c.1500hrs: Reinforced by a detachment from Fort Erie, Sheaffe launches an attack. By 1600hrs the fighting has ceased and the only Americans on the Canadian side of the Niagara are either prisoners or dead.

Battlefield environment

Queenston Heights ("the Heights") is actually a portion of the Niagara Escarpment. This escarpment runs predominantly east–west through the United States and Canada, with some breaks, for a length of 650 miles. The escarpment creates Niagara Falls, where the Niagara River (actually a fast-flowing 37-mile-long strait connecting Lakes Erie and Ontario) flows over it. Queenston is north of the escarpment, sitting at its foot. This village was prosperous before the war and was the northern end of the portage road used to ship goods around Niagara Falls. The village proper comprised some 100 houses, several of brick-and-stone construction. Queenston Heights (the escarpment) towers over the village, rising 200ft. The north face of the escarpment had been cleared of woods. On its river side, Queenston Heights rises some 300ft above the water as a nearly vertical cliff. The top of the escarpment was partially covered with old oak forest. The north face, a 200yd-wide strip at the top, and the land along the riverbank southward, were owned by the British Government for use by the military. A redan containing an 18pdr cannon and an 8in mortar had been built atop the Heights to fire across the Niagara. South and west of the government land on the escarpment's top were surveyed lots, some used as farmland and owned by local citizens. The fighting for Queenston Heights would cover the ground from the village to the woods on top of the escarpment.

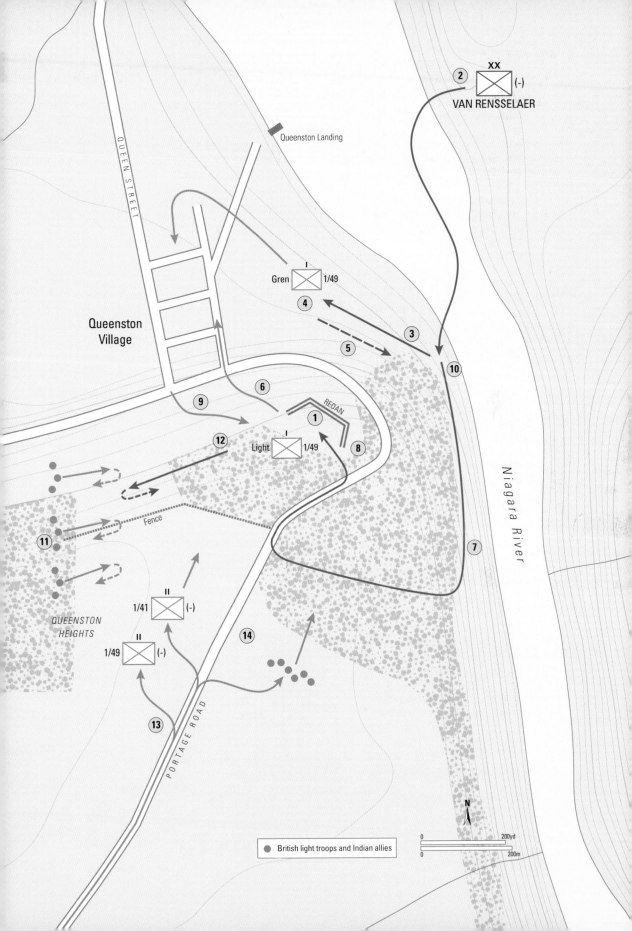

Queenston Landing

QUEEN STREET

Queenston Village

Queenston Heights

Fence

Portage Road

Niagara River

Redan

VAN RENSSELAER

XX (-)

Gren 1/49

Light 1/49

1/41 (-)

1/49 (-)

N

0   200yd
0   200m

● British light troops and Indian allies

INTO COMBAT

The loading site for the boats was an old portage landing a mile south of Lewiston. Loading began around 0330hrs, October 13. The first problem of the day for the amateur US forces was the failure to appoint an officer to control the embarkation, which allowed regular/militia jealousy to disrupt the plan. First to be loaded, as planned, were the regular artillerists. Colonel John Chrystie brought the five companies of the 13th Infantry (regulars) under his command to the loading site and proceeded to load the boats without regard for the militiamen. Colonel Van Rensselaer recognized the need to get the operation underway, so he ordered his militia subordinate to send the first wave's planned 150 militiamen across with the second wave. Van Rensselaer then joined the artillery detachment, crossing with them. The 13 boats moved out with around 300 men to start an invasion of Canada. The landing site was a small beach 500yd south of Queenston at the base of a 40ft rise.

The first wave landed around 0400hrs, its subsequent progress to the Heights and engagement in battle described by Captain John Wool of the 13th Infantry:

> The guard stationed on the Bank discovered us and fired into our boats before we reached the shore, but fled on our landing. As soon as we left the boats we ascended the bank and formed line fronting the heights. Being the senior officer in the absence of Col. Chrystie I took command of the detachment. At this moment Judge Advocate Lush arrived and informed me of the landing of Colonel Van Rensselaer and his party, with orders from the Colonel to "prepare for storming Queenston Heights." I informed him we were ready. In a few moments he returned with an order to march. We proceeded a few rods [1 rod=16.5ft] when I received an order to halt. This was at the foot or base of the heights — our right extending towards the Village of Queenston. Whilst thus waiting further orders the detachment was attacked on its right by a party of British from the Village of Queenston. Without waiting for orders from Colonel Van Rensselaer the detachment was immediately brought to bear on the enemy. A short but severe contest ensued. The enemy was repulsed, but not without the loss of six officers killed and wounded out of 11 or 12 present, besides a large proportion of non-commissioned officers and privates, all of the 13th U. S. Infantry. Of the officers, Lieut Valleau and Ensign Morris were killed, and Captains Wool, Malcolm and Armstrong and Lieut Lent wounded. (Letter in *New York Public Library Bulletin 9*, 1905)

The guard soon spread the alarm. Captain James Dennis, commander of the 1/49th Foot's grenadier company, marshaled the defenders of Queenston. The defense consisted of the 1/49th Foot's grenadier company and light company, four militia flank companies, and militia artillerymen, directed by six men of the Royal Artillery, with an 18pdr cannon and one 8in mortar in a redan atop the Heights and a 9pdr cannon at Queenston Landing. The light company, commanded by Captain John Williams, was on the Heights while Dennis's grenadier company and the militia flank companies were in and around the village. Notified of the Americans' landing site, Dennis led his grenadier

Major General Stephen Van Rensselaer commanded the defeated American force at Queenston Heights. He was far more effective as a politician, businessman, and philanthropist. He founded the Rensselaer School (now Rensselaer Polytechnic Institute) in New York in 1824. When he died in 1839 his estate was worth $101 billion in 2014 dollars. (Courtesy National Gallery of Art, Washington)

company and some militiamen toward the beachhead underneath the Heights. It was this force that met the Americans and engaged in the firefight described above by Wool. Finding the American fire heavy and effective, Dennis pulled his small force back to the village. Williams' light company deployed on the Heights and directed volleys against the Americans below them. The British artillery on the Heights and in Queenston fired into the darkness toward the American boats. At Vrooman's Point, 2,000yd downstream (north), a 12pdr and an 18pdr cannon joined in firing on the Americans but were ineffective at the long range.

Not all the American boats reached the landing site. Three boats, including one with Colonel Chrystie aboard, went off course and came under fire when off Queenston. Chrystie was wounded and directed the boats to return to the American side. British artillery soon identified the embarkation site and began firing at it. The Americans' plan collapsed as boats were damaged or lost and no one was in charge. The crossing became a free-for-all as American regulars and some militiamen boarded any boat they could to cross. The result was confusion as some officers crossed without their troops and troops from other units crossed without officers. One bright spot was that the two American 18pdr cannons at Fort Gray were able to silence the British 9pdr cannon at Queenston Landing.

As dawn broke around 0630hrs, Colonel John Fenwick of the Light Artillery led a group of regulars (artillerists and infantry) and part of a militia rifle company across the Niagara. Unfortunately, at least four and possibly as many as six boats steered north of the planned landing site and came under heavy fire from the British in Queenston. Fenwick's group landed at Hamilton Cove, about 1,100yd north of the first wave's beachhead, and were immediately engaged in an intense firefight with Dennis's force. Fenwick was wounded as he stepped ashore. One officer later reported that half his men were killed or wounded in the landing. The surviving Americans initially fought hard, but found the British defense too strong to overcome. Most of the Americans surrendered, including the wounded Fenwick, but a few managed to escape back to the US shore in one of the boats. British personnel at Fort George later reported seeing boats drifting downstream with bodies in them. Chrystie later estimated that over 100 regulars were lost in this failed movement.

The Hamilton Cove landing prompted Dennis to order Williams to pull the 1/49th Foot's light company off the Heights and join his force in Queenston, a move which left the artillery battery in the redan atop the Heights unsupported. Around 0630hrs the Americans captured the redan, as recounted by Wool in a letter:

> Shortly after the enemy had retreated Ju[d]ge Advocate Lush came and informed me that Colonel Van Rensselaer was mortally wounded, with orders from the Colonel to retire with the troops to the shore. As soon as it was light I repaired to Colonel Van Rensselaer and asked him what could be done? He replied he did not know. I remarked that some thing must be done soon or we would all be taken prisoners. His reply was that he knew of nothing unless we could take Queenston heights. Although wounded, a musket ball having passed through both my thighs, I offered to undertake the enterprise. It was no sooner communicated to such of the officers of the 13th able to march, consisting of, besides myself, Captain Ogilvie, Lieutenants Hugunin, Kearney, Car, Reab, and Sammons, than they rallied their troops, and with a small detachment of Artillery commanded by Lieutenants Gansevoort & Randolp[h] agreeably to the directions of Colonel Van Rensselaer, ascended the heights and captured the battery. (Letter in *NY Public Library Bulletin 9*, 1905)

More Americans crossed the Niagara and reinforced the troops on the Heights.

Brock arrived from Fort George around 0630hrs, in time to witness Fenwick's failed landing. Brock discussed the situation with Dennis and quickly gave directions. Reinforcements were ordered from Fort George and Chippawa, but it would take hours for these to arrive. Brock reacted to the loss of the artillery battery atop the Heights by deciding that it had to be retaken immediately. Without any reconnaissance, he gathered together about 50 men of the 1/49th Foot's light company and local militia and led them up the Heights. Without regard for himself, Brock, sword in hand, led the small party into the fire of Wool's 200 or so Americans, mostly men of the 6th, 13th, and 23d Infantry. Brock's general's uniform made him conspicuous and he was soon killed by American fire. His fall brought the counterattack to a complete halt. For the moment, it seemed as if the Americans had succeeded in capturing the Heights.

This depiction of Lieutenant-General Sir Thomas Picton, one of the Duke of Wellington's key subordinates in the Peninsular War and at Waterloo, suggests how distinctive in appearance Brock would have been on the front line at Queenston Heights. Although Brock would not have worn all the elements of full dress shown here, any US soldier would have recognized that the man they saw was an important officer and a high-value target. (National Museum & Galleries of Wales Enterprises Limited/Heritage Images/ Getty Images)

The fighting now became a series of exchanges between skirmishers as both sides waited for reinforcements and strengthened their positions. Wool remained in command of the American force on the Heights. Between 0800hrs and 0900hrs, Williams led elements of the 1/49th Foot's light company and local militia against Wool's position on the Heights. In an intense firefight the British force pressed the American position, but the advance stalled and then broke when Williams was wounded and the Americans advanced. Leaving 21 prisoners behind, the British force retreated, moving to Queenston.

By 1000hrs the Americans had secured the Heights and Queenston Landing on the Niagara, which made it easier to move troops across the river and evacuate the wounded. One 6pdr field gun was moved across and manually moved to the Heights. An estimated 1,300 men crossed the river. Major General Van Rensselaer placed Lieutenant Colonel Winfield Scott (of the 2d Artillery) in command on the Heights before 1100hrs. Scott later claimed that his effective force was just 125 regular infantrymen (from the 6th, 13th, and 23d Infantry), 14 regular artillerymen, and 296 assorted militiamen (other estimates have his force as high as 500 men). Scott describes the next phase of the battle in his memoirs using the third person:

> A pause ensued. The lieutenant-colonel rapidly reconnoitered the heights; took up a position for defense until joined by the great body of the forces remaining in camp at Lewiston; introduced himself and adjutant to his line of battle, and attempted to unspike the guns the enemy had left in the captured battery. While directing the latter operation the enemy's collected forces suddenly drove in our pickets, when regulars, volunteers, and Indians rushed upon our line of battle, which, intimidated, began to face about, and in a moment would have been in full retreat, but that the lieutenant-colonel, running back from the battery, by storming and free use of the sword, brought his whole line to face the enemy, and, in a charge to drive them beyond reach. (Scott 1864: 59)

This attack was carried out by Indians friendly to the British and a few Canadian militiamen totaling fewer than 100. Skirmishing on the Heights continued through the afternoon, and American troops performed well in this frontier fighting against an irregular opponent.

While this action atop the Heights was in progress, the 1/41st Foot's light company and a half-battery (two 6pdr cannons and a 4.5in howitzer) under Captain William Holcroft arrived from Fort George. Deploying north of Queenston, this small force pushed and scattered the Americans out of the village. Directing fire against any boat trying to reach Queenston Landing, Holcroft soon made it unusable for the American troops, who retreated to the Heights and the original landing site. Around 1300hrs Sheaffe arrived at Queenston from Fort George leading a column of reinforcements. This force was observed from the Heights by Scott, who now knew a stronger attack was coming: "Returning again to the chosen position our forces were reformed, and stood impatiently awaiting the arrival of reinforcements from the other side of the river; for the approach of a fresh column of the enemy from below could be plainly seen" (Scott 1864: 60).

Van Rensselaer also saw the approach of Sheaffe's force. With the New York militiamen having decided they could not legally be ordered out of their state, he sent a message to Scott informing him that there would be no reinforcements and ordering him to retreat.

Like Brock, Sheaffe decided that the Heights had to be retaken, but unlike Brock's impetuous charge, Sheaffe insisted on proper reconnaissance, careful planning, and the use of all his forces. He decided to make his attack from the south, which required marching his force west around the American position and out of the range of the American artillery on the eastern shore of the Niagara. He took with him about 650 men – regulars from both the 1/41st and 1/49th Foot and some militiamen – along with two militia-manned 3pdr cannons. Once south of the Heights, he waited for Captain Richard Bullock to arrive from Chippawa with 150 men of the 1/41st Foot, including the grenadier company, and 100 militiamen in flank companies. Bullock's small force arrived around 1500hrs. Sheaffe then deployed for the attack. The main British line, made up of soldiers of the 1/41st and 1/49th Foot, formed 400yd south of the American position. Regular and militia light companies, along with Indian allies, deployed in woods west of the Americans.

The 3pdr cannons opened the attack. The main body advanced, stopping to fire volleys at 100yd while light troops advanced, firing independently. With both sides firing, white smoke soon covered the battlefield. Under the cover provided by the smoke the British charged with fixed bayonets. Tired, low on ammunition, and scared, the American militiamen and some regulars broke and ran. The American commanders quickly decided to retreat, ordering the regulars to cover the retreat and delay the British. Morale collapsed as most

John Wool was commissioned a captain in early 1812. He then had a long and distinguished career: major of the 6th Infantry in 1815, brigadier general in 1841, and a divisional commander in the Mexican–American War (1846–48). In his late seventies, he commanded forces in the American Civil War, being promoted major general in 1862. (Anne S.K. Brown Military Collection, Brown University Library)

Queenston Heights

It is roughly 1600hrs, October 13, 1812. A US non-commissioned officer just behind the line is looking south. He sees soldiers of the British 1/41st Foot executing a bayonet charge 15yd before the oak woods in which the Americans are deployed. The British are in a two-rank line, with fixed bayonets. These men have opened the distance between themselves during the advance such that they are roughly 2ft apart. Behind the British and near the ground hangs a cloud of dense white smoke created by the burning black powder from volleys fired before the final charge. The soldiers of the 1/41st Foot have advanced through this smoke and are making a final rush.

Some 300yd beyond the charging British infantry are two 3pdr cannons obscured by smoke from both the infantry's musket fire and the artillery's cannon fire. The crews of the cannons are watching the advance as their infantry blocks the line of fire to the Americans. Directly in front of the observer are Americans of the 13th Infantry. These men are in a ragged line, firing at the British. On the ground around the Americans are dead and wounded men. Some American soldiers, shaken by the British fire, are already getting ready to fall back toward the north. These Americans are a shaky rearguard wanting to flee.

soldiers fled to the riverbank trying to escape the dreaded Indians. Some Americans held together; the 13th Infantry claimed to have held the line until the British reached the regiment with the bayonet. This finally broke the American resistance. Scott described the end: "The firings, on both sides, were deadly, and then followed a partial clash of bayonets. The Americans, by force of overwhelming numbers were pushed from the height … A surrender was inevitable. There was no time to lose. The enemy were gradually letting themselves down the precipice, which partially covered the Americans, near enough to render their fire effective" (Scott 1864: 61). Carrying a white flag, Scott was shot at several times before he was taken to Sheaffe. Accepting the surrender, Sheaffe ordered a ceasefire sounded at about 1600hrs.

A second American army had been defeated; out of an estimated 600 regulars and 800 militiamen who crossed the Niagara, losses were estimated at 500 killed, wounded, or drowned with 925 prisoners. British losses were 20 dead, 85 wounded, and 22 prisoners. Brock's death was a blow to the British, but their victory at Queenston Heights further demoralized the Americans and seemed to demonstrate the superiority of the British Army. Queenston Heights was actually Sheaffe's victory. Unfortunately for his memory, he was soon forgotten and Brock became immortalized in Canada for the useless heroics that resulted in his death.

Crysler's Farm

November 11, 1813

BACKGROUND TO BATTLE

The British had built up their strength in Canada during 1812 and early 1813 as best they could while still engaged in conflict with Napoleon's France. By fall 1813, seven battalions of British infantry (including a Canadian fencible battalion on the British establishment) and two foreign-recruited battalions had been added. There were 17 battalions of infantry in Canada by fall 1813. The British commander, Lieutenant-General Sir George Prévost, judged that Montreal and Quebec were key to maintaining Britain's position in North America. He viewed everything west of Montreal as expendable and believed that as long as he held these two settlements Britain would be able to retake any territory lost in the west. His strategy was therefore to avoid significant risks and maintain his forces intact.

In summer 1813 the Americans debated their strategy for the Lake Ontario–St. Lawrence River area. Three options were considered: occupy the Canadian side of the Niagara River; capture Kingston, Ontario; or move down the St. Lawrence River and capture Montreal. The Niagara option would not be decisive and would only move both armies into Ontario. Capturing Kingston would remove the Royal Navy's Lake Ontario base and was favored by the US Navy. Capturing Montreal would sever the British supply line for all their forces around the Great Lakes such as the Niagara region, Detroit, and farther west. The summer passed with no decision being made. The Americans concentrated their Niagara–Lake Ontario force near Sackett's Harbor across the lake from Kingston. By early October Major General James Wilkinson appears to have decided to attack Kingston.

A second American force invaded Canada from the Lake Champlain region. Under Major General Wade Hampton, a force of 4,000 men entered Canada along the Chateauguay River which flows northeasterly from New York and

The northern campaign of 1813 began with a number of successful but limited American attacks. One of these was the May 27 storming of Fort George on the Canadian side of the Niagara River near its mouth on Lake Ontario. The first wave of Americans was led by the ever-active Brigadier General Winfield Scott. (Anne S.K. Brown Military Collection, Brown University Library)

enters the St. Lawrence across from Montreal. Moving down the Chateauguay River, Hampton encountered a force of Canadian militiamen and fencibles on October 26. The resulting fight was won by the Canadians; casualties numbered a combined total of 20 killed and 39 wounded. Major John Wool later wrote: "no officer who had any regard for his own reputation, would voluntarily acknowledge himself as being engaged in it" (quoted in Lossing 1869: 648).

Wilkinson began his movement on October 16, but instead of attacking Kingston he moved toward Montreal. The St. Lawrence drops 200ft between Lake Ontario and Montreal, therefore his army's flotilla would have to pass through five rapids. Given the time of year, ice could soon form on the river, hampering movement and endangering boats. Wilkinson's flotilla of over 300 assorted river craft, schooners, and scows moved downriver. His force of 7,300 men was organized into five brigades, four numbered 1st through 4th and a fifth designated the Reserve Brigade.

At Kingston there were five battalions of British regulars and part of a sixth, one company of Royal Artillery, and assorted militia. The commander at Kingston, Major-General Francis de Rottenburg, veered between expecting an attack on Kingston or another cross-lake attack on York (modern-day Toronto), as had occurred in April. Prévost, concerned about Montreal, ordered De Rottenburg to form a brigade sized "corps of observation" to reinforce Montreal should the Americans move down the St. Lawrence. When Wilkinson's force was sighted moving toward Montreal, De Rottenburg ordered Lieutenant-Colonel Joseph Morrison, commander of the 2nd Battalion, 89th Foot at Kingston, to lead the force sent downriver. The corps of observation consisted of the 1/49th Foot and the 2/89th Foot.

By November 10, the Americans had reached the beginning of the Long Sault Rapids. Throughout their advance downriver, they had been harassed by British and Canadian forces along the shore and by British river gunboats to their rear. Now, the corps of observation from Kingston, reinforced by regulars and militiamen from posts the Americans passed, was near. There was constant skirmishing between pickets and it was clear that a British

force of some size was at hand, perhaps waiting to cut off and destroy an American rearguard. The advance guard under Brigadier General Jacob Brown, composed of the 2d and Reserve brigades, had been moving along the northern shore of the St. Lawrence, eliminating British positions and protecting the flotilla. Wilkinson's orders for passing the rapids were:

> General [Jacob] Brown will prosecute his march with the troops yesterday under his command, excepting two pieces of artillery and the 2nd [Light] Dragoons; who, with all the well men of the other brigades, except a sufficient number to navigate the boats are to march under orders of Brigadier General [John] Boyd. ... Brigadier-General Boyd will take the necessary precautions to prevent the enemy who hangs on our rear, from making a successful attack; and if attacked is to turn and beat them. (Quoted in Armstrong 1840: 14)

The night of November 10/11 was cold and wet and the soldiers passed the miserable hours until dawn in the open. The Americans anticipated that the 11th would be spent marching past the rapids.

A view of the battle of the Thames, October 5, 1813. A US Navy victory on Lake Erie allowed the US Army to recapture Detroit and invade Canada. British and Indian forces tried to stop advancing Americans at the Thames River in western Ontario, but a larger force of veteran Kentucky militiamen was victorious. (Library of Congress, LCCN 91790904)

Dating from 1815, this illustration also depicts Major General William Harrison's victory at the battle of the Thames, October 5, 1813. (Anne S.K. Brown Military Collection, Brown University Library)

1 *c.***1330hrs:** British light troops under Major Frederick Heriot slowly withdraw while delaying the advance of the Americans through the woods between the campgrounds of the two armies.

2 *c.***1330hrs:** The American 4th Brigade leads the advance through the woods followed by the 1st Brigade. The two brigades move in a single column composed of regimental close columns that present a frontage of one company in three ranks. Behind these two brigades the 3d Brigade follows.

3 **1330hrs:** The British main force is drawn up for battle on Crysler's Farm awaiting the American advance.

4 *c.***1400hrs:** As the Americans reach the edge of the woods, their commander, Brigadier General John Boyd, sees the British position and orders the 4th and 1st brigades to move through the woods north of the fields and outflank the British.

5 **1400–1430hrs:** Heriot's light troops continue to skirmish and delay the 4th and 1st brigades' column in the woods.

6 *c.***1415hrs:** The 21st Infantry is detached from the 4th Brigade and advances into the field in line formation, then advances parallel to the large column in the woods.

7 *c.***1500hrs:** The 4th Brigade advances out of the woods and begins to deploy into line with the 1st Brigade directly behind it.

8 *c.***1500hrs:** Lieutenant-Colonel Joseph Morrison orders the 2/89th Foot to deploy and fire into the 4th Brigade as it tries to deploy. British musketry and artillery fire, for which the dense American column is a perfect target, soon shatter both the 4th Brigade and the 1st Brigade following it.

9 *c.***1500hrs:** The 3d Brigade arrives, deploys its three regiments into line, and advances against the troops of Captain George Barnes and Lieutenant-Colonel Thomas Pearson holding the west side of the First Gully. British troops under Barnes and Pearson fall back to the Second Gully and stand their ground.

10 *c.***1515hrs:** The 4th and 1st brigades break and retreat, leaving the British free to concentrate on the 21st Infantry and arriving 3d Brigade.

11 *c.***1530hrs:** The 1/49th and 2/89th Foot advance to oppose the Americans' right flank. The 2/89th Foot engages the 21st Infantry in a firefight that results in the US regiment retreating as it runs low on ammunition.

12 *c.***1545hrs:** The 3d Brigade, its right flank uncovered, retreats to the woods.

13 *c.***1545hrs:** The US artillery finally arrives and engages the British in order to cover the US infantry's withdrawal.

14 *c.***1600hrs:** A squadron of the 2d Light Dragoons makes an unsupported charge against the 1/49th and 2/89th Foot and is shot up by the British infantry. Morrison decides not to pursue the retreating Americans and the battle ends.

Battlefield environment

Today Crysler's Farm Battlefield is under the waters of the St. Lawrence Seaway, flooded by the Moses-Saunders Power Dam in 1958. The battlefield itself was about 2,000yd from the American army's camp around Cook's Tavern. Between the camp and battlefield was a second-growth wood which stretched from the river to a swampy pine forest to the north and through which the Americans had to advance. Some 200yd west of the woods was a large ravine formed by a muddy creek, and west of this lay the battlefield proper.

The battlefield itself was roughly 1,500yd east to west and 900yd north to south, bounded on the north by a swampy pine forest and on the south by the St. Lawrence. The field was flat farmland, partly plowed, and partly covered in fall wheat. This plateau 25ft above the river provided unobstructed views and fields of fire. It was intersected by two small ravines or gullies near the river. The first gully was 250yd west of the large ravine and the second was 250yd west of the first one. The gullies were steep-sided and muddy, and slowed movement along the river road. Several wood rail fences ran through the fields, but these were easily taken down. At first the fences impeded movement, but they provided no protection from artillery or musket fire. Although skirmishing occurred in the woods, the battle was decided on a near-perfect field for British regulars to maneuver and fight upon.

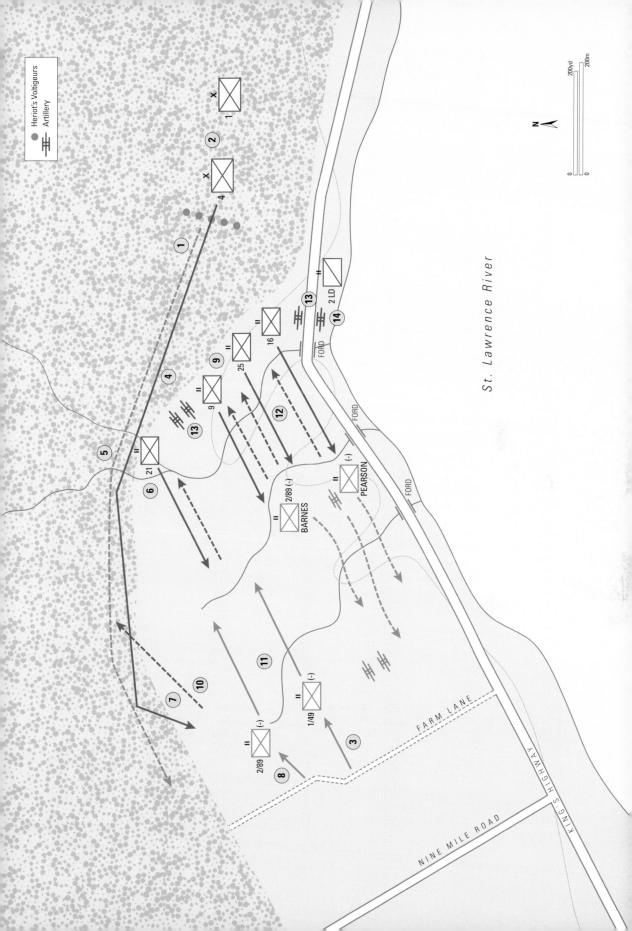

Heriot's Voltigeurs
Artillery

St. Lawrence River

N

200yd
200m

X
1

2

X
4

1

4

5

6
21

13

9

9

25

13
16

13

2 LD

14

FORD

12

FORD

PEARSON

BARNES
2/89 (-)

FORD

10

7

11

1/49 (-)

3

2/89 (-)

8

FARM LANE

NINE MILE ROAD

KING'S HIGHWAY

INTO COMBAT

The Americans were up and formed to march in the direction of Montreal early on October 11. Brigadier General John Boyd commanded the three brigades near Crysler's Farm: his own 1st, the 3d, and 4th. All three were understrength due to detachments and sickness. The brigades did not start their march that morning, however, and confusion reigned in the camp. During Wilkinson's subsequent court martial, Boyd recalled that:

> During the fore-part of the day, a variety of verbal orders, were brought to him [Boyd] by the aides of the commander in chief ... These were, generally countermanded, before they were executed.
>
> The troops were paraded, in an open space, and between them and where the enemy were supposed to be, was a piece of woods. Between 12 and 2 o'clock, during a violent storm, and the troops having been nearly forty-eight hours under arms; the witness, impatient for orders, rode down to the bank, and received from General Swift [Colonel Joseph Gardner Swift, Chief Engineer of the Northern Army], an order written with a pencil, directing him, to put the troops in motion, in twenty minutes, or as soon as four pieces of artillery should be landed, and dragoons dismounted to draw them. Before this time had expired, one of his videttes rode up and informed him, of the approach of the enemy. (Quoted in Wilkinson 1816: 84–85)

Morrison and his British–Canadian force were deployed west of Boyd's campsite along a 700yd front between the river and the woods. Their deployment was described by Morrison:

> The ground being open the troops were thus disposed, the flank companies of the 49th Regiment, the detachment of the Canadian Fencibles with one field piece, under Lieut.-Colonel Pearson on the right, a little advanced on the road; three companies of the 89th Regiment under Captain Barnes with a gun formed in echelon with the advance on the left supporting it. The 49th and 89th thrown more to the rear, with a gun, formed the main body, and a reserve extending to the woods on the left, which were occupied by the Voltigeurs under Major Heriot. (Quoted in Cruikshank 1907: 8.169)

Observing the Americans in a state of apparent indecision during the morning, Morrison ordered a forward movement between noon and 1300hrs. This was carried out by Major Frederick Heriot with three companies of Canadian Voltigeurs. Advancing through the woods that separated the two forces, the Voltigeurs, essentially regulars in all but name, soon encountered American outposts. Heriot's advance was what American videttes reported to Boyd, who ordered Brigadier General Robert Swartout to attack the British force with his 4th Brigade. This brigade was in the rear of the column that had been formed to march by the rapids. The other brigades, also in the column, were ordered to support Swartout.

The 4th Brigade's 21st Infantry led the movement into the woods followed by the 14th and 11th. These units, in a column of march intended to move to the east, about-faced and moved to the west. The brigade had approximately

900 effectives. The Canadian Voltigeurs fired and retreated into the woods. A sharp skirmish started with the Voltigeurs, who operated in dispersed two-man teams as prescribed by British light-infantry doctrine, carefully selecting targets and attempting to ensure each shot hit its mark. The Voltigeurs were supported by a small contingent of pro-British Mohawk Indians, who were experts in forest fighting. Heriot's force fought a delaying action against the superior number of Americans and gave ground slowly.

The 3d Brigade, about 900 strong, under Brigadier General Leonard Covington moved out after the 4th Brigade and formed into three regimental columns made up of the 9th, 25th, and 16th Infantry regiments from north to south. Each regimental column had a frontage of one company. The 3d Brigade advanced into the woods on a 500yd front with its southern flank resting on the St. Lawrence and the 4th Brigade on its northern flank. Boyd's 1st Brigade, now under Colonel Isaac Cole, numbering roughly 450 men of the 12th and 13th Infantry, advanced in column behind the 4th Brigade.

Heriot's detachment of roughly 200 men was pushed through the woods (about 1 mile in width) by some 2,000 Americans. As the Americans moved forward, however, they became disorganized by the woods and the eagerness of the men to get involved in the fighting. Hearing the exchanges of gunfire between the 4th Brigade and Heriot's detachment, the 3d Brigade's men began to rush forward. By about 1400hrs the Americans had reached the western edge of the woods and found a deep ravine in front of them. Across the ravine were open fields bordered on the north by more woods into which most of Heriot's men moved to continue harassing the advancing Americans.

The Americans were surprised to see the main British force of regulars in front of them. Boyd now knew he was not facing the harassing militiamen as he originally thought, but a British force that he claimed was 2,000–2,500 men. Their position appeared strong, as Boyd later wrote: "The enemy had judiciously chosen his ground among the deep ravines which everywhere intersected the extensive plain, and discharged a heavy and galling fire upon our advancing columns" (quoted in Cruikshank 1907: 8.177). Boyd attacked. He ordered Swartout's 4th Brigade, followed by Cole's 1st Brigade, to move through the woods along the northern edge of the fields to turn the flank of the British line. Eleazer Ripley, at the time a colonel commanding the 4th Brigade's 21st Infantry, recalled that:

> There were no lines formed; the troops were not in order of battle, but in columns to march down the river. The artillery was not stationed, nor the cavalry posted, with a view to attack the enemy.
>
> There was no simultaneous movement of corps and brigades in order of battle; but one of the whole column towards the enemy; they marched at various points. (Quoted in Wilkinson 1816: 142)

The 21st Infantry advanced in a two-rank line through the fields south of the woods. The rest of the 4th Brigade – the 14th and 11th Infantry – moved through the woods in a column of companies, forming a mass approximately 30 men wide and 15 deep. The 1st Brigade's 12th and 13th Infantry followed in a similar formation.

This US Army sergeant is wearing the 1812 regulation uniform. After a year of war, sergeants who learned their duties replaced those who did not. Field duty, as well as combat, filtered out incompetents and dilettantes who obtained discharges, deserted, or were assigned to easy duties in garrisons or depots. (Culture Club/Getty Images)

As the 4th Brigade slowly advanced through the woods, it again encountered the Voltigeurs fighting a delaying action. The 21st Infantry was slowed to nearly the same pace as the column in the woods by the muddy plowed terrain and the need to tear down wood rail fences encountered in the field. The British commander saw that a flank attack was being conducted. Morrison responded by ordering his left flank, comprised of the five companies of the 2/89th Foot, to change its alignment by 45 degrees so that its line faced the Americans coming out of the woods. As the leading American regiments entered the open field, their officers tried to deploy them in a proper firing line. American discipline did not hold up, however, as the leading men started to fire individually and failed to deploy properly. The British remained silent, as they did against French attacks, and maintained a disciplined line. They waited until Morrison gave their commander the order to fire. The 2/89th Foot opened fire: first the three right-hand companies fired a volley, followed by the two left-hand companies. The 11th and 14th Infantry were caught, as had been so many French units in the Peninsular War, trying to deploy from column to line, which was further complicated because the two regiments were in a single close column of companies – a march formation – instead of individual French-style attack columns. The already shaky American units began to fall apart. The British now started firing by platoon volleys, sending an almost continuous hail of musket balls into the crowded formation.

British artillery pieces opened fire on the Americans once they were at the tree line. British 6pdr field guns started firing spherical case, or shrapnel, against the massed columns of Americans. Each round contained 27 musket balls that were propelled toward the ground when the shell exploded. Manned by well-trained Royal Artillerymen under Captain Henry Jackson, the 6pdrs inflicted heavy casualties on the Americans and disrupted their columns. Outside of musket range and with no American artillery firing on them, the gunners could work as if they were on an artillery training field.

As the 4th Brigade's men broke to escape the superior British fire, the two regiments of the 1st Brigade came out of the woods behind them in a single company-wide column. Immediately the two brigades became intermixed and uncontrollable. Only Ripley's 21st Infantry, south of the woods, was

A watercolor showing a gunner of the Royal Artillery, *c.*1812. Being members of a technical branch, artillerymen needed skills not found in the infantry. Handling artillery, and firing it, would have soiled a gunner's uniform quickly. Except for parade grounds in major garrisons, it is unlikely that most gunners would be so immaculately dressed. (Hulton Archive/ Getty Images)

in line. The 21st Infantry remained in line as the other four regiments fell back under musket and shrapnel fire. Ripley was farther from the British line than the ill-fated brigade columns and he tried to get his regiment to advance in an attempt to reduce the pressure on his comrades. He soon saw, however, that many of his men had left their positions in line to find whatever little cover the field provided and to fire individually without orders; but because the distance between the 21st Infantry and the British was beyond effective musket range, his men wasted their ammunition. Once his men started falling back as they ran out of ammunition, the regiment began wavering. Ripley decided to withdraw to the woods behind him and resupply his men. Their retreat ended the firefight on this segment of the field and the British left flank was now safe. Colonel John Harvey, Morrison's chief of staff, described this action in a letter the next day:

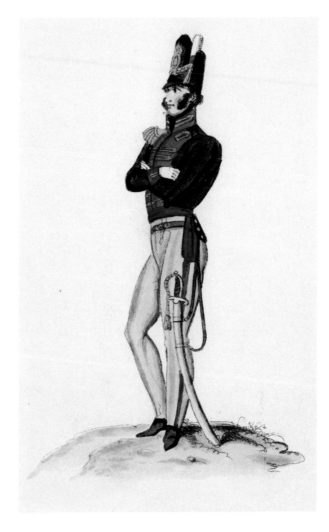

> I then recommended to Colonel Morrison to advance the line in echelon of battalions. On arriving within musket distance the enemy's columns halted, and commenced a heavy but irregular fire, which our battalions returned with infinitely more effect by regular firing. The superiority of this fire, of platoons and wings, aided by that of our three field-pieces, which were admirably served, gave, after a severe contest, the first check and repulse to the enemy, and his columns fell back... (Quoted in Edgar 1890: 253)

A watercolor showing an officer from the Royal Artillery, c.1812. The officers of the Royal Artillery were well trained and highly professional. These men did not purchase commissions; instead they were all graduates of the Royal Military Academy at Woolwich. Artillery officers were considered specialists by the rest of the Army, as were engineer officers. (Hulton Archive/Getty Images)

While the 1st and 4th brigades were being repulsed, Covington's 3d Brigade moved forward against the British right near the St. Lawrence. The 9th, 25th, and 16th Infantry formed in line at the edge of the woods before entering the open fields. Opposing them were two detachments; the Advance (flank companies of the 1/49th Foot and two companies of Canadian fencibles) next to the St. Lawrence under Lieutenant-Colonel Thomas Pearson and three companies of the 2/89th Foot under Captain George Barnes deployed to the left and in echelon to Pearson. The 3d Brigade had to cross a muddy ravine 20ft deep which disrupted its formations. Colonel Cromwell Pearce's 16th Infantry was trying to re-form after crossing when it was hit by a well-delivered first volley from Pearson's detachment. This fire was reported as destructive by survivors and the mortally wounded Covington, who turned his brigade over to Pearce.

Crysler's Farm

American view: We see the view from inside the American 21st Infantry. The commander of the rightmost company of the 21st Infantry is in the first rank of the rightmost file. To his left, he sees that his company is in alignment with the rest of his regiment. To his front he sees five companies of the British 2/89th Foot advancing in echelon of companies. Each British company is in close order of two ranks.

Between the three companies on the British right, which is the Americans' left, and the two on the British "left" is the 2/89th Foot's regimental color party. On the company commander's left, he notes that the most advanced company has stopped moving. This company is roughly 100yd from the 21st Infantry and will provide the guide point for the other companies to form line upon.

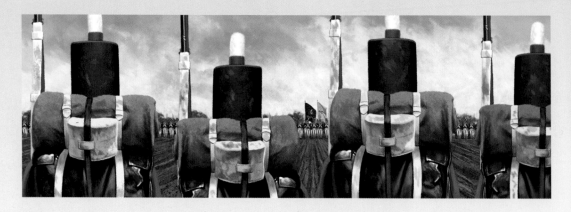

British view: We see the view from inside the British 2/89th Foot, stationed on the British right. To the immediate right of the senior officer of the 2/89th Foot's fourth company is the regimental color party. Beyond these are the three companies of the right wing in echelon. To his front, he can see the ten companies of the 21st Infantry arrayed in a two-rank line with

the regimental color party in the center of the line. This American line mimics a British ten-company regiment and appears to be in good order. What the company commander does not know is that the 21st Infantry has trained using the British regulations. One factor he quickly notices that favors his company is that it overlaps the Americans in front of him on his left.

Flintlock muskets firing black powder generated large clouds of dense white smoke and could quickly foul the barrel. With hundreds to thousands of muskets firing in volleys the field would become obscured by this smoke after a few minutes, resulting in increased levels of anxiety and confusion. (Mark Wilson/Getty Images)

Climbing out of the ravine, the 16th Infantry formed line and returned fire. The regiment was joined on its right by Colonel Edmund Gaines' 25th Infantry. Soon the volleys from the two American regiments took effect: several officers went down and Pearson's horse was shot out from under him. Confusion began to grow in the British ranks and Pearson ordered a retreat. With the 9th Infantry on the 25th Infantry's right, the 3d Brigade now advanced, threatening to turn the British right flank.

Having driven back the 1st and 4th brigades, Morrison quickly reacted and reported of the enemy: "His efforts were next directed against our right, and to repulse this movement the 49th took ground in that direction in echelon, followed by the 89th; when within half-musket shot the line was formed under a heavy but irregular fire from the enemy" (quoted in Cruikshank 1907: 8.169). The Americans opened up at maximum range and soon the opposing lines were engaged in a musketry duel. Again the British were supported by their 6pdr field guns. The contest was decided by ammunition supply; the Americans had 38 rounds per man compared to 60 rounds each for the British. After 15 minutes, the inexperienced 25th Infantry broke and ran to the rear. The 16th Infantry was engaged with Pearson's Advance, which was now supported by Barnes' three companies of the 2/89th Foot. When ammunition ran low, the 16th Infantry retreated to the woods in good order, but in doing so the 9th Infantry was left on its own. Under fire from the 1/49th and 2/89th Foot as well as artillery, it too retreated. The main infantry battle had lasted roughly an hour and a half.

Eleazer Ripley

Eleazer Wheelock Ripley was born in Hanover, New Hampshire, April 15, 1782. He graduated from Dartmouth College in 1800 and then practiced law. He was elected to the Massachusetts House of Representatives in 1810 and to that state's Senate in 1812. In August of that year he was commissioned lieutenant colonel and assigned to organize the new 21st Infantry recruited in Massachusetts and Maine. In March 1813 he was promoted to colonel of the regiment. Ripley drilled his regiment to fight in the two-rank British firing line, which it used at Crysler's Farm. The 21st Infantry performed better than its fellow regiments. While still in need of improvement, its conduct and Ripley's leadership were among the few things that went well for the Americans.

Ripley was among the new crop of brigadier generals promoted in April 1814 and was assigned to command the 2d Brigade in Major General Jacob Brown's force on the Niagara front. Ripley's old 21st Infantry was part of this brigade. He led his brigade at the battle of Lundy's Lane (having missed Chippawa) on July 25, 1814, and following the wounding of both Brown and Scott took temporary command of Brown's division. He was wounded at Fort Erie on September 17.

After the war, Ripley was posted to Louisiana in 1815. He left the US Army in 1820 and returned to politics. He was elected to the House of Representatives from Louisiana's Second District in 1835 and served until his death on March 2, 1839.

Eleazer Ripley as a colonel. Although a political appointee, Ripley took his regimental command duties seriously and was soon recognized as one of the US Army's better officers. (Hulton Archive/Getty Images)

Joseph Morrison

Joseph Wanton Morrison was born in New York, May 4, 1783, the son of the deputy commissary general of the British Army then occupying New York at the end of the American Revolutionary War (1775–83). He started his military career in the British Army as an ensign at the age of ten, but did not see active service until 1799 as a lieutenant in the 2/17th Foot. In April 1800 he became a captain and in June 1805 transferred to the 2/89th Foot. In November 1809 he was promoted to lieutenant-colonel of the 1st West India Regiment in Trinidad. In July 1811 he exchanged back to the 89th Foot, taking command of the 2nd Battalion. He led the battalion to Canada, arriving at Halifax October 13, 1812. The 2/89th Foot was sent up the St. Lawrence River to Kingston, Ontario, in 1813.

As the Americans moved along the St. Lawrence toward Montreal, Morrison was chosen to command a small brigade, or "corps of observation," assembled at Kingston to follow and harass them. When the Americans turned to fight on November 11, 1813, he ably maneuvered them onto terrain of his choosing that maximized his small force's combat power. Crysler's Farm was Morrison's victory and undoubtedly saved Montreal from the threat of attack.

After the war, Morrison rose to the rank of brigadier-general in 1824 and was placed in command of an expedition against Burma. During this campaign he caught malaria and had to give up his command due to sickness. He died at sea on February 15, 1826, while returning to England from India.

Lieutenant-Colonel Joseph Morrison was a thoroughly competent professional officer, a product of the Duke of York's military reforms. (© McCord Museum M401)

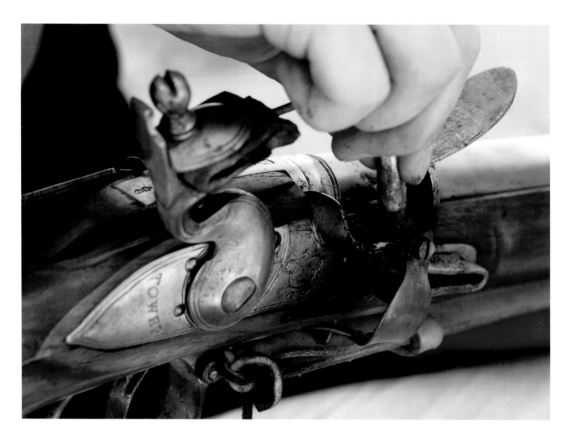

A War of 1812 reenactor cleans his musket. The coarse black powder used during the early 19th century quickly fouled muskets with ash and unburnt grains of powder. Fouled muskets could misfire. Because the first volley fired in an action came from cleaned muskets, it was frequently the most effective. Officers would try to control when their men fired so that they could deliver the first volley at an opportune moment. Victory in a firefight often went to the unit with the best fire discipline; early in the war this would usually be the British. (Mark Wilson/ Getty Images)

American artillery finally entered the fight in the form of two 6pdr field guns of the Light Artillery and four 6pdrs of the 2d Artillery; a squadron of the 2d Light Dragoons also joined in. The rest of the fight was succinctly described by Morrison:

The 49th was then directed to charge the gun posted opposite to ours, but it became necessary when within a short distance of it to check the forward movement in consequence of a charge from their cavalry on the right, lest they should wheel about and fall upon their rear, but they were received in so gallant a manner by the companies of the 89th under Captain Barnes and the well directed fire of the artillery that they quickly retreated, and by an immediate charge of those companies one gun was gained. The enemy immediately concentrated their force to check our advance, but such was the steady countenance and well directed fire of the troops and artillery, that about half-past four they gave way at all points from an exceeding strong position, endeavoring by their light infantry to cover their retreat, who were soon driven away by a judicious movement made by Lieut.-Colonel Pearson. The detachment for the night occupied the ground from which the enemy had been driven ... (Quoted in Cruikshank 1907: 8.169–70)

Morrison reported British losses as 22 killed, 148 wounded, and nine missing. American reports listed 102 killed and 237 wounded with no missing. The British counted 75 American prisoners. Once again, a small British force had defeated a larger American army. The US forces soon crossed to the south side of the St. Lawrence and withdrew, saving Montreal from an attack.

This monument was commissioned to commemorate the British–Canadian victory over the Americans at Crysler's Farm. It was erected on the battlefield in 1895. The site was flooded in 1958 by the construction of the Moses-Saunders Power Dam as part of the St. Lawrence Seaway project. The monument was relocated to the Upper Canada Village historic site in Morrisburg, Ontario. (Toronto Star Archives/Toronto Star via Getty Images)

Chippawa

July 5, 1814

BACKGROUND TO BATTLE

By late 1813 President James Madison and Secretary of War John Armstrong had seen the lack of ability in most of their senior officers; Major Generals Henry Dearborn, James Wilkinson, Wade Hampton, and Morgan Lewis had all failed in 18 months of war. Drastic changes in the US Army's senior leadership were needed: Hampton resigned, Dearborn and Lewis were sidelined to coastal-defense posts, while Wilkinson was relieved and charged with neglect of duty and drunkenness. Although acquitted in January 1815 by a court martial, he was effectively unemployable for the rest of the war.

New generals were promoted for 1814, among them Major Generals George Izard and Jacob Brown, both promoted January 24, 1814. Izard was a prewar regular, having served in the engineers and artillery. He had served capably under Hampton in the failed 1813 campaign. Brown had been a New York militia general; his successful defense of Sackett's Harbor in early 1813 resulted in a Regular Army brigadier general's commission. His performance as commander of Wilkinson's advance guard in the 1813 St. Lawrence campaign led to further promotion to major general. Izard commanded the "Right Division of the 9th Military District" at Lake Champlain and Brown commanded the "Left Division of the 9th Military District" covering the Niagara border and the St. Lawrence River to Ogdensburg, New York.

The Niagara frontier became the center of gravity for Brown's operations in 1814 because neither the Royal Navy nor the US Navy could achieve superiority on Lake Ontario. As his principal subordinates, Brown had three newly promoted brigadier generals: Winfield Scott, Eleazer Ripley, and

Edmund Gaines. Scott and Ripley commanded the 1st and 2d brigades of the Left Division while Gaines commanded the defenses of the Sackett's Harbor naval base on Lake Ontario. Brown placed Scott in charge of training his main body, composed of the 9th, 11th, 21st, 22d, 23d, and 25th Infantry. Scott described his task in his memoirs using the third person:

> The major-general, though full of zeal and vigor, was not a technical soldier: that is he knew but little of organization, tactics, policy, etc., etc. He therefore charged Scott with the establishment of a camp of instruction at Buffalo, and the preparation of the army for the field by the reopening of the season …
>
> Nothing but night or a heavy snow or rain was allowed to interrupt these exercises on the ground – to the extent, in tolerable weather, of ten hours a day, for three months … [Scott's]… own labors were heavy and incessant. Take for illustration *infantry tactics*; the basis of instruction for cavalry and artillery as well. As Government had provided no text book Brigadier-General Scott adopted for the army of the Niagara, the French system, of which he had a copy in the original, and there was in camp another, in English – a bad translation. He began by forming the officers of all grades, indiscriminately into squads and personally instructed them in the schools of the soldier and company. They then were allowed to instruct squads and companies of their own men …
>
> The evolutions of the line, or the harmonious movements of many battalions in one or more lines … were next daily exhibited for the first time by an American army, and to the great delight of the troops themselves, who now began to perceive

Brigadier General Edmund P. Gaines was one of the 1814 class of new generals. He had been in the Regular Army since 1801, rising from lieutenant to major general. After Major General Jacob Brown was wounded in the summer of 1814, Gaines took command of the Niagara front. He remained a general, serving until his death in 1849. (Hulton Archive/Getty Images)

why they had been made to fag so long at the drill … Confidence, the dawn of victory, inspired the whole line. (Scott 1864: 120–21)

For the first time the Americans would go into battle with a well-trained and -disciplined force under officers who had been selected based on their battlefield performance rather than their political connections. Rounding out the division was the 3d Brigade under Brigadier General Peter Porter (New York State Militia), composed of 600 Iroquois warriors, a small company of US-born men who had lived in Upper Canada, and one regiment of Pennsylvania volunteers. Four companies of regular artillery supported the division.

The British troops on the west side of the Niagara River were part of the "Right Division" of the British Army in Upper Canada. This division was a territorial command responsible for the British troops deployed west of Kingston, Ontario. It was scattered in eight locations along the shore of Lake Ontario, the Niagara, and farther west. On June 22, 1813, the "Right Division" included all or part of the 1/1st, 1/8th, 1/41st, 100th, and 103rd Foot. Although the last two regiments had been raised in 1804 and 1808 respectively, all were well trained, well disciplined, and highly confident in their ability to defeat the Americans on an open battlefield. Commanding the "Right Division" was Major-General Phineas Riall, who arrived in Canada in late 1813.

In March 1814, the fighting in Europe ended with Napoleon's abdication and first exile. Britain could now transfer numbers of experienced soldiers to North America. Both Britain and the United States were weary, however, of an expensive war that offered little to the majority of their people. For Britain, the end of Napoleon's Empire removed the threat to national existence. Britain's landowning taxpayers and merchants wanted peace, which would bring reduced taxes and expanded trade with the United States. The US economy had been wrecked by the British blockade, however, which had reduced foreign trade to almost nothing. Both countries decided to seek a peace treaty. Military operations in 1814 would be carried out with the overriding concern of influencing negotiations, which finally began in August.

The US Government directed the 9th Military District's Left Division to cross the Niagara and capture Burlington Heights in Ontario. This would cut British supply lines to the Western region and their ability to supply Britain's Indian allies. Officials in Washington, DC, knew that the US Army could not capture York or Kingston unless the US Navy under Commodore Isaac Chauncey defeated the Royal Navy under Captain James Yeo on Lake Ontario. Both Chauncey and Yeo were extremely cautious, however, and each refused to engage in battle unless he was sure of winning. Therefore, Brown's Niagara offensive became the primary focus of the Northern theater in the summer of 1814.

Winfield Scott, depicted here in 1814 as a major general, became Commanding General of the Army in 1841 and served until forced to retire in 1861. During the Mexican–American War, he commanded the army that captured Mexico City. At the outbreak of the American Civil War, he conceived the "Anaconda Plan" for defeating the Confederacy by securing the Mississippi River and blockading or capturing their ports. The eventual Union victory contained most of the features of his plan. (Library of Congress, LC-USZ62-25559)

MAP KEY

1 Morning: US forces in their camp are harassed by sniper fire from Indian allies of the British operating within woods to the west.

2 c.1400hrs: Brigadier General Peter Porter's 3d Brigade of Pennsylvania volunteers and Iroquois warriors advance through the woods and drive the British allies back toward the Chippawa River.

3 c.1500hrs: Porter's command is met by Lieutenant-Colonel Thomas Pearson at the head of British regular light infantry, Canadian militiamen, and Indians, and is driven back.

4 c.1500hrs: Major-General Phineas Riall orders his British regulars to advance across the Chippawa and form for battle in the open terrain. Because of limited space, the 1/8th Foot is deployed on Riall's right behind the line formed by the 1/1st and 100th Foot.

5 c.1600hrs: Brigadier General Winfield Scott's 1st Brigade advances in column under British artillery fire and deploys in line.

6 c.1630hrs: Riall orders his infantry to advance and attack Scott's 1st Brigade.

7 c.1645hrs: With the British approximately 100yd away, Scott orders his 1st Brigade to fire. The British stop and a close-range musketry battle begins.

8 c.1650hrs: After a few volleys, Scott sees the flank of the 100th Foot is exposed and orders his 11th Infantry to pivot and attack the British flank.

9 c.1700hrs: The 25th Infantry pushes through the woods and engages the 1/8th Foot from the tree line, firing into the British regiment's flank and preventing it from supporting the 100th Foot.

10 c.1710hrs: Suffering heavy casualties, especially among his officers, and with the Americans showing no sign of retreat or panic, Riall orders a fighting withdrawal to Chippawa village.

Battlefield environment

The Niagara River turns west for about 3 miles before it reaches the massive Niagara Falls. Along this stretch, the Chippawa River (now called the Welland River) enters the Niagara on the Canadian shore. The Chippawa was 70yd wide and unfordable at its junction with the Niagara. On the northwest side of the Chippawa was the village of the same name. The village contained about 20 residences and several storehouses. It was the southern terminus of the portage route around Niagara Falls and was connected by a wagon road with Queenston, the northern terminus. On the southeast side of the Chippawa was the main battlefield. This was an area of flat fields bounded on the north and east by the bank of the Niagara, to the west and southwest by a dense forest, and to the southeast by Street's Creek. A tongue of the forest reached to about 250ft of the Niagara blocking the line of sight between the bridges across the Chippawa and Street's Creek. There was a distance of approximately 1,500yd between the end of the tongue of forest and Street's Creek and 800yd between the main forest and the Niagara; the area was covered with grass about 3ft high. This field was the perfect setting for a fight between infantry forces using classic linear tactics. While the main bodies of the two sides dueled in the open field, light troops, militiamen, and Indian allies skirmished in the adjacent forest.

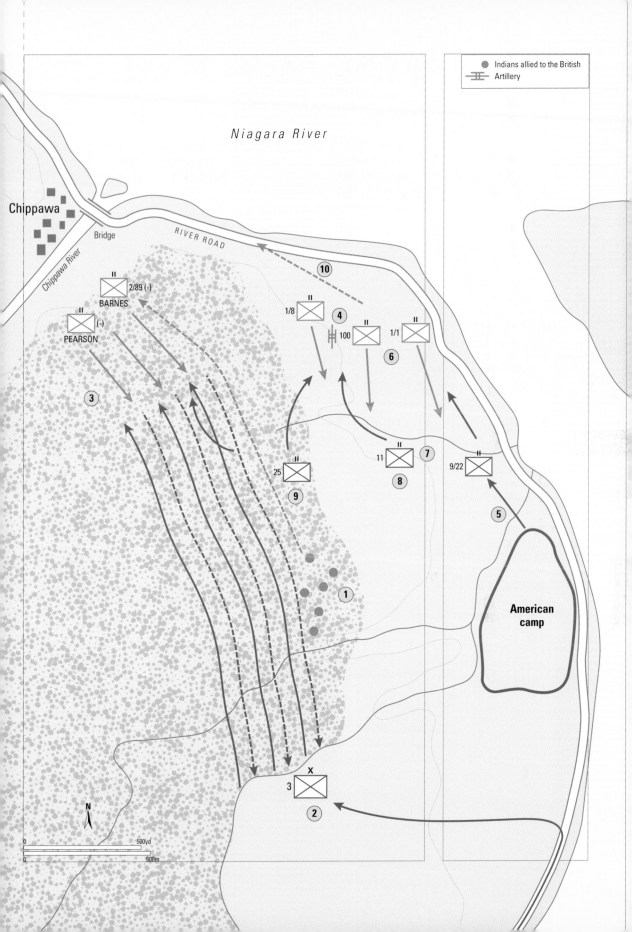

Niagara River

Chippawa

Bridge

Chippawa River

RIVER ROAD

Indians allied to the British

Artillery

10

II 2/89 (-)
BARNES

II (-)
PEARSON

3

II 1/8

4

100

II 1/1

II

6

II
11

7

II 9/22

II
25

9

8

5

1

American camp

X
3

2

N

0   500yd
0   500m

INTO COMBAT

Brown's Left Division started crossing the Niagara after midnight on July 3 to attack Fort Erie, and four days later he wrote:

> On the 2d instant I issued my order for crossing the Niagara river, and made the arrangements deemed necessary for securing the garrison of fort Erie. On the 3d that post surrendered at 5 P. M.
>
> On the morning of the 4th, brigadier general Scott, with his brigade and a corps of artillery, was ordered to advance towards Chippawa, and be governed by circumstances; taking care to secure a good military position for the night. After some skirmishing with the enemy, he selected this plain with the eye of a soldier, his right resting on the river, and a ravine being in front. At 11 at night, I joined him with the reserve under general Ripley, our field and battering train, and corps of artillery under major Hindman. General Porter arrived the next morning with a part of the New York and Pennsylvania volunteers, and some of the warriors of the Six Nations. (Quoted in Brannan 1823: 368)

Riall learned of the crossing made by Brown's Left Division later in the morning and directed troops from Fort George to move south to the Chippawa River. In addition, Riall ordered the 1/8th Foot to sail from York to Fort George. He reported to his superior, Lieutenant-General Sir Gordon Drummond, on July 6:

> I have the honor to inform you that the enemy effected a landing on the morning of the third inst., at the ferry opposite Black Rock, having driven in the picket of the garrison of Fort Erie. I was made acquainted with this circumstance about eight in the morning and gave orders for an immediate advance to Chippawa of five companies of the [1st] Royal Scots to reinforce the garrison of that place. … Lieut.-Colonel Pearson had moved forward from thence with the flank companies of the 100th, some militia and a few Indians, to reconnoiter their position and numbers. He found them posted on the ridge parallel to the river near the ferry and in strong force. I received information from Major Buck that they had also landed a considerable force above Fort Erie. In consequence of the King's Regiment, which I had reason to expect the day before from York, not having arrived, I was prevented from making an attack that night. (Quoted in Cruikshank 1897: 31)

The morning of July 5 found the armies in close proximity. The American main body was encamped about 1 mile southeast of Chippawa village. Pickets were deployed between the camp and the Chippawa River and in the woods west of the camp. The British – still awaiting the 1/8th Foot, which arrived during the morning – were in and around the village with allied Indians and Canadian militiamen in the woods scouting the American camp. Soon the two sides' pickets and scouts were engaged in a desultory exchange of fire. British-allied Indians moved through the woods and fired at targets in the American camp. According to Brown, "Early in the morning of the 5th, the enemy commenced a petty war upon our pickets, and, as he was indulged, his presumption increased; by noon he showed himself on the left of our extensive line, and attacked one of our pickets …" (quoted in Brannan 1823: 368).

Riall received reports from his scouts and, still unaware of Fort Erie's fall, thought he was facing a small covering force. Late that morning, after the 1/8th Foot had arrived at Chippawa, Riall conducted a personal reconnaissance of the American position and decided to attack. The bridge over the unfordable Chippawa was damaged and had to be repaired before his main force and its supporting artillery could cross, with the result that it was after 1500hrs before the British main body was ordered to move south of the Chippawa. The three battalions of foot stayed in march column on the river road while their light companies, along with militiamen and Indians, were placed under the command of Lieutenant-Colonel Thomas Pearson and formed up in the fields south of the Chippawa.

In the mid-afternoon, Brown, annoyed by the firing from the woods, ordered Porter to take his 3d Brigade and clear the woods west of the camp. Porter recalled that at 1400hrs he

> … formed the whole corps … into single line or Indian file half-a-mile in rear of our camp, with the Indians towards the woods, and then marching into the woods in a line at right angles with the river … I had only to halt [and] by simply facing to the right, form my line of battle looking towards Chippawa, and presenting a front of three-fourths of a mile in length and one man deep. (Quoted in Cruikshank 1897: 369)

Porter's 3d Brigade outnumbered and overlapped the British-allied Indians and militiamen and drove them back through the woods. At the northern edge, Porter encountered the three regular British light companies, the disciplined volleys of which drove Porter's men back.

Riall directed his force across the repaired bridge over the Chippawa and through a gap between the woods and the Niagara. Lieutenant-Colonel George Hay's 100th Foot was deployed on the left (east) next to the river and Lieutenant-Colonel John Gordon's 1/1st Foot was on the right. Two 24pdr field guns and one 5.5in howitzer (under Lieutenant Richard Armstrong) were positioned between the 100th Foot and the Chippawa while three 6pdr field guns (under Lieutenant Edmund Sheppard) were positioned to the right of the 1/1st Foot. Riall placed Major Thomas Evans' 1/8th Foot on the right in echelon and partly overlapping the 1/1st Foot because there was not enough space between the Chippawa and the woods for all three battalions.

Brown, who was on the plain north of the American camp, heard the volleys of the British light companies and saw the cloud of dust raised by Riall's main body. He sent a message to Scott to form up his 1st Brigade and advance. Brown then rode south to order Ripley's 2d Brigade to join Scott, who had assembled his brigade that afternoon to conduct brigade-level drill. He now put his men in motion. They had to cross Street's Creek on a narrow bridge and soon came under British artillery fire. The 1st Brigade was wearing gray jackets instead of regulation blue; Scott insisted on uniformity in clothing and was unable to get the blue. Gray being the only color available, Scott had outfitted his entire brigade in gray.

The Americans' march in column and subsequent deployment into line under British artillery fire led to one of the legends of Chippawa. Scott wrote in his memoirs: "General Riall, who had dispersed twice his numbers the winter before, in his expedition on the American side, said 'It is nothing but a body of Buffalo militia!' But when the bridge was passed in fine style, under his heavy fire of artillery, he added with an oath 'Why these are regulars!'" (Scott 1864: 129). Scott's account was the first time this tale was printed; true or not, the maneuvering of Scott's 1st Brigade was noted by British officers and soldiers who saw that these Americans were not the untrained amateurs of the last two years.

Once across Street's Creek, Scott deployed his brigade: the combined 9th and 22d Infantry under Major Henry Leavenworth took up position on the right (next to the Niagara) and the 11th Infantry under Colonel Thomas Campbell (soon to be wounded and replaced by Major John McNeil) was on Leavenworth's left. Seeing Porter's men running along the wood line to the rear, Scott ordered the 25th Infantry under Major Thomas Jesup into the woods to secure the 1st Brigade's left and move around the British right flank. Scott's attached artillery, one company under Captain Nathan Towson with two 6pdr field guns and one 5.5in howitzer, was placed between the Niagara and the 9th/22d Infantry's line.

The plain south of the Chippawa now held two nearly equal brigade-sized forces; the British with roughly 1,400 infantry and six field guns, and the Americans with 1,350 infantry and three field guns, the latter of which were reinforced by four more field guns during the fight. Initially the deployed lines were outside musket range of each other so the battle became an artillery fight. The field guns deployed next to the Niagara engaged each other while the British field guns deployed on their right targeted the 25th Infantry. Since the range was 500yd or more, round shot was used by Sheppard's 6pdrs against the 25th Infantry. The duel between Armstrong's and Towson's field guns soon led to one British 24pdr and the American howitzer being put out of action.

It was now around 1600hrs and Riall could see only Scott's 1st Brigade before him. Still believing that most of the Americans were besieging Fort Erie, Riall was confident that superior British discipline would prevail over the Americans in a stand-up fight with the sides being equal in numbers.

He decided to attack. Orders were issued for the 1/1st and 100th Foot to charge the Americans to their front and the 1/8th Foot to advance toward the right to hit the 25th Infantry on Scott's left. It was approximately 1630hrs when the three British battalions, deployed in the traditional two-rank line, launched their advance. Once Riall issued the order to advance, he stationed himself behind the line to try to maintain his situational awareness of the whole battle. The British battalion commanders knew their job, and intended to use combined fire and shock to defeat the enemy.

The British moved forward, maintaining silence as they advanced, withholding their fire until they were within close musketry range. The first volley, properly loaded before advancing, would be fired on order. Two or three volleys were to be delivered, followed by an advance with fixed bayonets. These tactics had worked for years for British infantry, as they had during the previous two years against the Americans. As the British advanced they came between Sheppard's 6pdrs and the Americans, forcing the British artillery to cease fire. Armstrong and Towson, reduced to two field guns each, continued to fire at each other by the Niagara.

As Scott watched the silent advance of his opponent, he saw the British line separate into two components, the 1/1st and 100th Foot in line coming straight at him and the 1/8th Foot in a separate line somewhat behind the first two. He decided to move the left of the 11th Infantry forward, pivoting its alignment, so as to be able to fire down the flank of the 100th Foot. He next ordered Towson to fire his field guns on the advancing British infantry instead of their artillery. With infantry as their target, Towson's field guns switched to canister.

During the battle of Chippawa, Scott ordered the 11th Infantry under Major John McNeil to advance upon the overlapped British line in order to fire into its flank. Contrary to legend, the British did not break. Instead, unable to advance and suffering heavy casualties, they slowly retreated in order. (Anne S.K. Brown Military Collection, Brown University Library)

Bayonets of the late 18th and early 19th centuries were sharpened steel blades up to 18in long with a triangular cross section. They were attached to the musket using a socket mount that fitted around the barrel. The blade was offset, allowing the musket to be fired and reloaded with the bayonet attached. (The New York Historical Society/Getty Images)

Once the British were 150–200ft from his line, Scott ordered the 9th/22d and 11th Infantry to fire. The 1/1st and 100th Foot halted and returned fire. It was 1645hrs and Scott reported: "Majors Leavenworth and McNeil made prompt dispositions to receive the charge. The fire of these corps (including the artillery) produced a prodigious effect on the enemy's ranks. That of Major McNeil's was most effective from the oblique position which his corps judiciously occupied" (quoted in Cruikshank 1897: 46). Many Americans used aimed fire, targeting those British officers they could see through the smoke. The 100th Foot lost two officers killed and 11 wounded, leaving four officers on duty by the end of the action; the 1/1st Foot had one officer killed and nine wounded. Hay and Gordon, the two British battalion commanders, attempted to get their men to move forward, but the volume of musketry from the Americans was such that the British soldiers were unable to advance. Hay and Gordon, both wounded during this time, were taken off the field. Despite losses, both sides stood their ground exchanging fire. For the British this was a new experience. The Americans were standing firm in a duel of infantry line versus infantry line and appeared as solid as any line could. As men fell on both sides, the soldiers closed ranks, continued to fire, and remained at their posts.

The battle was decided by the clash between the 1/8th Foot and the 25th Infantry. Riall ordered Evans to take his 1/8th Foot into the fight on the far right of the British line. After forcing Pearson's light companies to retreat from the woods west of the battlefield, however, the 25th Infantry marched out of those woods on the British right flank. The regiment then fired three volleys and charged to attack the 1/8th Foot. McNeil saw the 25th Infantry's advance and ordered his 11th Infantry forward. Leavenworth soon followed by advancing the 9th/22d Infantry as well. Additional American artillery arrived; two 6pdr field guns and one 5.5in howitzer commanded by Captain John Ritchie and one 12pdr field gun commanded by Lieutenant James Hall. These guns were placed between the 11th and 9th/22d Infantry and began firing canister into the British. The British line was flanked, shelled by six artillery pieces firing canister, and its losses were mounting, especially among officers singled out by American marksmen. With two of his battalion commanders out of action, Riall ordered a retreat.

Only 25 minutes had passed since Scott's brigade fired their first volley. The Americans held the field as the British withdrew north, crossed the Chippawa, and returned to their camp. By holding the field, the Americans claimed victory. The human cost for the Americans was 58 killed, 241 wounded, and 19 missing. The British lost 148 killed, 321 wounded, and 46 missing.

For the British regulars this had been a new experience, for they had failed to rout an American force. Moreover, the despised Americans had maneuvered and fought like regular soldiers. The British survivors had personally seen that the war near Niagara had changed, and the change was not to their advantage. For the Americans of Brown's little army, they now knew they could stand against the British.

Analysis

The three actions described provide an opportunity to examine the interrelationship between doctrine, training, discipline, leadership, and experience. A military unit is a collection of humans, each of whom experiences fear, fatigue, comradeship, elation, and pride among the many human emotions. This collection of men can quickly disintegrate into a panicked mob. A unit is held together by discipline, training, and the individuals' knowledge of what to do in combat. Unit pride, determination not to let down one's friends and comrades, and respect for – and trust in – their leaders are more motivating to soldiers during combat than lofty ideas of patriotism and national goals. If any of these is lacking, a unit can quickly fall apart under the stresses of battle.

British and Canadian regulars in North America were among the most professional soldiers in the world in 1812. Even units that had served in Canada without recent battle experience were far more ready for combat than their American opponents. Having trained and drilled to common doctrine, junior leaders and enlisted men knew what they were to do when words of command were issued in the furnace of combat, even when these came from officers with whom they were unfamiliar. Experience of combat during 1812 and 1813 showed the British soldiers that their training and drill made them superior to the Americans on the battlefield. American officers and men saw how British training and discipline allowed their opponents to defeat them. Many Americans decided that they too needed to attain the same military standards as their enemy if they were ever to prevail on the battlefield.

The war started with the US Army being a collection of ill-trained units with an officer corps that was selected for political loyalties rather than military competency or education. The heavy reliance on state militias meant that initially, large numbers of troops could be mustered. These militiamen, however, were mostly untrained, undisciplined, frequently ill-equipped, and prone to refusing orders that they disagreed with. The early-war regulars

This photograph from 1900 shows Queenston village and Queenston Heights as viewed from Lewiston, New York. The Niagara Escarpment, the Heights, stretches to the west, dominating the ground at its foot. On top, the monument to Major-General Brock dominates the scene. (Library of Congress, LCCN 2016794104)

were as green as the militiamen. Compounding these problems was the lack of a single unifying doctrine. Militiamen generally used the American Revolutionary War-era doctrine of Baron von Steuben, while the regulars used a mix of French- and sometimes British-inspired doctrine. As the war continued, the Regular Army became progressively better; incompetents were weeded out (the second-most senior general was awaiting court martial during the 1814 campaign), or left the service, and younger men, educated by experience and personal study (such as Winfield Scott), rose to positions of command. Veteran enlisted soldiers became NCOs and taught recruits their trade while setting examples of soldierly conduct in camp, drill, and battle. Doctrine emerged, fostered by competent leaders who focused their efforts on training in the essentials required for combat while also explaining the need for discipline to their men. By 1814 the Americans usually relegated militiamen to defense behind fortifications or used them as skirmishers and guerrilla fighters in woods and broken terrain when faced by British regulars.

The battle of Queenston Heights in October 1812 was the first battle of the war. The US Army was not ready to conduct an offensive against Canada, however. Political expediency, naive views of warfare, conflicts of ego, amateurism, and delusional faith in poorly trained and recently recruited soldiers, both regulars and militiamen, led to defeat. Major General Stephan Van Rensselaer of the New York State Militia was placed in overall command, but he was a Federalist politician and an opponent of Republican President James Madison. Some felt that Van Rensselaer was being set up for failure in order to remove him from being a candidate for future political office. The senior regular general, Brigadier General Alexander Smyth, was a Republican political loyalist who refused to take orders or cooperate with Van Rensselaer, thus fragmenting the American force on the Niagara line. Planning was defective: no objective other than crossing the Niagara River and securing Queenston Heights was designated; only 13 boats were collected for crossing the Niagara; and no officer was placed in charge of superintending loading of the boats. No plans were made to resupply the troops once they crossed, and no clear chain of command was designated. Compounding these problems was the fact that many militiamen, faced with the perils of combat, discovered "constitutional" grounds to refuse to cross into Canada. They decided that they were only required to serve within New York and could not be ordered to invade Canada, thus providing a convenient excuse for cowardice. Regular officers developed a great distrust of militiamen from this battle and capable ones learned the importance of training and drill on the battlefield.

The British had a clearly defined unified command structure. The regulars knew their jobs thoroughly and the Canadian militia was defending its own land. Major-General Isaac Brock's quick reaction to the American landing bought time, but his impetuous charge at the head of a small number of men cost him his life. The regimental- and company-level British officers at Queenston Heights took charge, however, and conducted a stout defense. Brock's next in command, Major-General Roger Sheaffe, carefully brought up his forces, examined the American position, and deployed his men accordingly. Circling the Heights, Sheaffe launched his attack from the high ground south of Queenston and defeated the Americans. Queenston Heights was a victory of professionals over amateurs. To the British, the battle confirmed their belief in their Army and its doctrine.

The battle of Crysler's Farm in November 1813 was another American defeat. Although Major General James Wilkinson's American force was composed of regulars, it still proved inferior to its British (and Canadian) opponents. The regular regiments at this battle had been in existence since June 1812, but the men that remained in service with these regiments were no longer green recruits. Junior officers and NCOs were learning their jobs,

Dead, Major-General Brock became a hero to the British and Canadians, who built this monument to honor him. The real victor, however, was his subordinate, Major-General Roger Sheaffe, who methodically organized his attack, collecting all available resources, and efficiently defeated the Americans. Unfortunately, Sheaffe has been forgotten by popular history. (Library of Congress, LCCN 2016797504)

and their field-grade officers greatly improved. The Americans still suffered from a lack of a common battlefield doctrine, however. Many units had trained to variations of French-inspired drill, while at least one regiment, the 21st Infantry, had been trained by its commander to the British regulations. Most general officers in the force advancing down the St. Lawrence River performed poorly. Brigadier General John Boyd, left to command at Crysler's Farm, proved to be unsuited to the task. He failed to coordinate the three brigades under his charge into a concerted attack and quickly lost control of his force, presenting the outnumbered British with the opportunity to defeat separate detachments one at a time.

The British forces at Crysler's Farm were led by a sound professional, Lieutenant-Colonel Joseph Morrison. Crysler's Farm may have been his first battle, but 14 years in the British Army had turned him into a well-trained and capable field officer. His troops were British and Canadian, all well trained, highly disciplined, experienced, and led by competent subordinates. The Americans found themselves outmatched at the points of contact despite a numerical superiority of more than 2:1 on the field. The American defeat was a simple case of senior leadership failure. Once more an outnumbered British force defeated a larger enemy force, confirming the British belief in their superiority over the Americans.

The battle of Chippawa in July 1814 showed that significant improvements had been made in the US Army. These began in early 1814 with a purge of general officers. Although all of the major generals had failed except for William Harrison in the Michigan theater, 2½ years of war had brought forward a group of brigadier generals such as Jacob Brown (promoted to major general) and colonels such as Winfield Scott (promoted to brigadier general) who had shown competence in command. Also, many junior officers and enlisted men had shown spirit and willingness to learn. Learning lessons from being defeated at the hands of the British, these men set about solving the problems that had led to failures and building a better-trained and more effective force in the coming campaign. The result was evident on July 5, when nearly equal forces of British and American regulars met on an open field and fought a musket duel in lines. The British retired, leaving the Americans in possession of the field and claiming victory. The British commander reported he was greatly outnumbered and forced to withdraw. In fact, he was not outnumbered; the British had encountered American regulars who were now their equals in leadership, training, and morale. This fight between two small brigades was summed up by the historian Henry Adams:

> The battle of Chippawa was the only occasion during the war when equal bodies of regular troops met face to face, in extended lines on an open plain in broad daylight, without advantage of position; and never again after that combat was an army of American regulars beaten by British troops. Small as the affair was, and unimportant in military results, it gave to the United States Army a character and pride it had never before possessed. (Adams 1891: 45)

The days of assured easy British victories against Americans were over. The US Army had been taught how to stand and fight as regulars in the hard school of combat, and their teachers were the best in the world – the British Army.

Aftermath

On July 25, 1814, the British and American Niagara commands fought again at the battle of Lundy's Lane north of Chippawa, and once again they fought close-range musket duels while standing their ground. Both sides claimed victory, but Lundy's Lane was in fact a bloody draw. Through late summer and early fall 1814 the fighting along the Niagara River continued with increasing casualty tolls. As long as the US Navy and Royal Navy squadrons on Lake Ontario played a cautious game of avoiding a major battle, neither side could gain a decisive advantage in the region.

On Lake Champlain the British launched an offensive from Montreal with reinforcements from Europe, but the lack of land transportation assets forced the British to use lake shipping for supply. Both sides built naval squadrons on Lake Champlain and this offensive hinged on the navies. On

Three weeks after Chippawa, British and American forces met again on the Canadian side of the Niagara at the battle of Lundy's Lane, or Niagara. A hard-fought battle between infantry lines left many casualties and no clear victor. The Niagara front drifted to a stalemate in fighting around Fort Erie. (Anne S.K. Brown Military Collection, Brown University Library)

A British amphibious force was able to capture and burn Washington, DC, on August 24, 1814. This was part of a raiding campaign within Chesapeake Bay. The British did not occupy Washington, DC; they withdrew to their ships the following day. The raid showed that the United States could not be defeated like a European power. (Library of Congress, LCCN 2007683564)

This fanciful print purports to show the British capture of Washington, DC. The British carried out amphibious raids along the Atlantic seaboard during the War of 1812, the largest being in Chesapeake Bay during the summer of 1814. While a European opponent would have responded differently, the capture of the US capital on August 24, 1814, did not yield any strategic benefit to the British. (© CORBIS/Corbis via Getty Images)

September 9, 1814, the two squadrons met in combat at Plattsburgh, New York. The Americans defeated the Royal Navy and the British Army quickly retired to Canada.

Peace negotiations had already started in the summer of 1814. A large part of the British mercantile class wanted peace, trade with America, and reduced taxes. Britain was tired after over 20 years of war against Revolutionary and Napoleonic France. The diplomatic situation in Europe was unsettled after Napoleon's abdication on April 11, 1814. Many in the British Government were focused on the Congress of Vienna where the victors were trying to establish a new balance of power and viewed the war with America as a sideshow. Peace was agreed to in Ghent in Belgium, and the Treaty of Ghent was signed on December 24, 1814. This was unknown in America, however, where the battle

A major British offensive down the Lake Champlain corridor in 1814 failed when a US Navy squadron under Commodore Thomas Macdonough defeated its Royal Navy rival on the lake. British supply depended on lake transport and American control of Lake Champlain meant the British army could not advance. (Library of Congress, LCCN 2012645359)

The battle of New Orleans was fought January 8, 1815, just over two weeks after the signing of the Treaty of Ghent on December 24, 1814. The British suffered heavy casualties attacking entrenched Americans, who were mostly Tennessee, Kentucky, and Louisiana militiamen with a few regulars. These militiamen were veterans of years of frontier warfare, and their victory restored public belief in the militia. (Library of Congress, LCCN 96513344)

of New Orleans on January 8, 1815, resulted in heavy losses to British troops attacking fortifications manned by a mix of US Army regulars and combat-experienced frontier militiamen. The fortifications were located behind the Rodriguez Canal, which was flooded to a depth of 5–6ft. The attack failed with British casualties of 285 killed, 1,265 wounded, and 484 captured or missing. The Americans suffered 13 dead, 30 wounded, and 19 captured or missing. This last-minute American victory that saw veteran militiamen deployed in the best possible conditions against regulars quickly became mythologized and was used to re-assert the value of state militias to defend the nation.

A depiction of the battle of New Orleans, showing the death of the British commander, Major-General Sir Edward Pakenham. (MPI/Getty Images)

Once the war ended, the US Army was reduced in size and its regiments consolidated and reorganized. The fates of the regiments that fought in the three actions above were various. The 6th, 16th, 22d, and 23d Infantry were incorporated into the new 2d Infantry; the 14th became part of the new 4th Infantry; the 9th, 13th, and 21st were absorbed into the new 5th Infantry; and the 11th and 25th went into the new 6th Infantry. Other War of 1812 regiments were consolidated into new 1st, 3d, and 7th Infantry regiments. The 12th Infantry and others were to become part of a new 8th Infantry, but the 8th was not organized. At the time of writing, War of 1812 battle honors are carried by the US Army's 1st through 7th Infantry regiments.

Since 1815, the British regiments that fought at Queenston Heights, Crysler's Farm, and Chippawa have been through two centuries of regimental restructuring and reductions. Only one of the regiments has completely disappeared from the British Army, however: the 100th Foot, renumbered in 1816 as the 99th Foot, but disbanded in 1818. Today the 1/1st Foot's honors are carried by The Royal Regiment of Scotland, the 1/8th Foot's by The Duke of Lancaster's Regiment, the 1/41st Foot's by The Royal Welsh Regiment, the 1/49th Foot's by The Rifles, and the 2/89th Foot's by The Royal Irish Regiment.

UNIT ORGANIZATIONS

British infantry

British Army regiments could have one or multiple battalions. If a single battalion, the unit would be called by its regimental designation, e.g. 100th Foot. In regiments with multiple battalions the unit would be designated with a battalion number, e.g. 2/89th Foot, which indicated the 2nd Battalion of the 89th Regiment of Foot.

Regardless of the number of battalions in a regiment, all British line battalions were organized into ten companies. These included a grenadier company, a light company (designated "flank" companies), and eight "center" companies. The grenadier company took up position as the rightmost company and the light company as the leftmost company when the battalion deployed in line. The eight center companies were stationed between the grenadier and light companies when in line.

The grenadier company was composed of the strongest and steadiest soldiers, who received extra pay. They were equipped like the soldiers of the center companies because grenades (hand bombs) were no longer used. The light company consisted of physically tough and intelligent soldiers who could be relied upon to operate effectively on the battlefield with less supervision. The light company was tasked with scouting and skirmishing and also received higher pay.

The British Army had several different manpower schemes for infantry battalions. The number of corporals and privates ranged (on paper) from 400 to 1,200 in increments of 200 men. Numbers depended on how many increments of one corporal and 19 privates were assigned to the battalion's ten companies. A sergeant was assigned to each increment.

The battalion was commanded by a lieutenant-colonel assisted by two majors, an adjutant, a quartermaster, and three NCOs. Company officers were one captain, one lieutenant, and one ensign. An additional lieutenant was added to companies in battalions with 1,000 or more men.

American infantry

The US Army started with three different Congressionally mandated infantry-regiment structures that varied (on paper) between 800 and 2,000 men and from one to two battalions in a regiment. In June 1812 the US Congress realized this was a problem and legislated a single regimental organization. A regiment was now composed of ten companies and formal battalions no longer existed within the regiment.

The US Army did not adopt the concept of flank companies as found in the British Army. There were no elite grenadiers or specialized light infantry. All American companies were intended to be multipurpose, capable of performing light-infantry duties as well as standing in a regimental line of battle.

The regiment was commanded by a colonel supported by a lieutenant colonel, major, adjutant, quartermaster, and paymaster. A regimental medical staff consisted of a surgeon and two surgeon's mates. Regimental headquarters included a sergeant major, quartermaster sergeant, and two musicians. Each company had one captain, one first lieutenant, one second lieutenant, and one ensign. A company also had four sergeants, six corporals, two musicians, and 90 privates. In March 1813 Congress added a second major to the regiment and a third lieutenant and another sergeant to each company. On paper a regiment at full strength would count 1,091 men.

American rifle regiments were organized as infantry, but with 68 privates per company. Because they frequently fought as infantry, artillery companies also need to be mentioned. An artillery company was authorized one captain, a first lieutenant, a second lieutenant, and four sergeants. The Light Artillery had 68 enlisted men per company, the 1st Artillery had 56 men per company, and the 2d and 3d Artillery had 95 men per company. The 1814 artillery consolidation set company strength at 100 men.

ORDERS OF BATTLE

Queenston Heights, October 13, 1812

British and Canadian forces
Regulars at Queenston: 1/49th Foot (184); 1/41st Foot (10); Royal Artillery (6)
Militias at Queenston: 5th Lincoln (100); 2nd York (80); 3rd York (30)
From Fort George (Major-General Isaac Brock): 1/41st Foot (210); Royal Artillery (33); 1st Lincoln, 4th Lincoln, and 1st York (130); militia artillery (10); Indians (100); unidentified regulars and militiamen (138)
From Chippawa (Major-General Roger Sheaffe): 1/41st Foot (150); unidentified militiamen (100)
Artillery: one 18pdr cannon, one 18pdr carronade, one 12pdr cannon, one 9pdr cannon, and two 6pdr cannons, manned by Royal Artillery and militia artillery

American forces (Major General Stephen Van Rensselaer)
Regulars: 13th Infantry (260); detachment from 6th and 23d Infantry (240); detachment from 1st, 3d, and Light Artillery serving as infantry (110)
New York State Militia: elements of 16th, 17th, 18th, 19th, 20th, and Hopkins's regiments and Rifle companies (c.700)
Supporting artillery (on US side of Niagara River): two 18pdr cannons, three 6pdr field guns, and one unidentified mortar, manned by 2d Artillery and New York State Militia

Crysler's Farm, November 11, 1813

Corps of Observation (Colonel Joseph Morrison)
Regulars: 1/49th Foot (382); 2/89th Foot (384)
Provincials: two companies of Canadian fencibles (108); three companies of Canadian Voltigeurs (150); Provincial Light Dragoons (12)
Mohawks (30)
Artillery: Royal Artillery (63), manning three 6pdr field guns

American forces (Brigadier General John Boyd)
1st Brigade: 12th Infantry (225); 13th Infantry (225)
3d Brigade: 9th Infantry (300); 16th Infantry (225); 25th Infantry (375)
4th Brigade: 11th Infantry (300); 14th Infantry (125); 21st Infantry (425)
2d Light Dragoons (150)
Artillery: detachments from the 2d Artillery and Light Artillery (100), manning six 6pdr field guns

Chippawa, July 5, 1814

British forces (Major-General Phineas Riall)
Regulars: 1/1st Foot (500); 1/8th Foot (400); 100th Foot (460); troop 19th Light Dragoons (70)
Militia: 2nd Lincoln (200)
Indians (300)
Artillery: Royal Artillery (70), manning three 6pdr field guns, two 24pdr field guns, and one 5.5in howitzer

US forces actively engaged (Major General Jacob Brown)
1st Brigade: 9th/22d Infantry (549); 11th Infantry (416); 25th Infantry (354)
3d Brigade: 5th Pennsylvania (militiamen/volunteers) (540); Iroquois (386)
Artillery: Towson's Company (89), manning two 6pdr field guns and one 5.5in howitzer; Ritchie's Company (96), manning two 6pdr field guns and one 5.5in howitzer; gun crew from Biddle's Company, manning one 12pdr gun

BIBLIOGRAPHY

Adams, Henry (1891). *History of the United States During the Second Administration of James Madison, Vol. 2*. New York: Charles Scribner's Sons.

Armstrong, John (1840). *Notices of the War of 1812, Vol. 2*. New York, NY: Wiley & Putnam.

Brannan, John (1823). *Official Letters of the Military and Naval Officers of the United States During the War with Great Britain*. Washington City: Way & Gordon.

Chartrand, René (1998). *British Forces in North America 1793–1815*. Men-at-Arms 319. Oxford: Osprey Publishing.

Cruikshank, E.A., ed. (1897). *The Documentary History of the Campaign Upon the Niagara Frontier, in the Year 1814*. Welland: Tribune Office.

Cruikshank, E.A., ed. (1900). *The Documentary History of the Campaign Upon the Niagara Frontier, in the Year 1812*. Welland: Tribune Office.

Cruikshank, E.A., ed. (1907). *The Documentary History of the Campaign Upon the Niagara Frontier, in the Year 1813*. Welland: Tribune Office.

Edgar, Matilda (1890). *Ten Years of Upper Canada in Peace and War 1805–1815*. Toronto: William Briggs.

Graves, Donald E. (1994). *Redcoats and Grey Jackets: The Battle of Chippawa, 5 July 1814*. Toronto & Oxford: Dundurn Press.

Graves, Donald E. (1999). *Field of Glory: The Battle of Crysler's Farm, 1813*. Toronto: Robin Bass Studio.

Katcher, Philip (1990). *The American War 1812–1814*. Men-at-Arms 226. Oxford: Osprey Publishing.

Kochan, James L (2000). *The United States Army 1812–1815*. Men-at-Arms 345. Oxford: Osprey Publishing.

Latimer, Jon (2009). *Niagara 1814: The final invasion*. Campaign 209. Oxford: Osprey Publishing.

Lossing, Benson J. (1869). *The Pictorial Field-Book of the War of 1812*. New York: Harper & Brothers.

Malcomson, Robert (2003). *A Very Brilliant Affair: The Battle of Queenston Heights 1812*. Annapolis, MD: Naval Institute Press.

Rules and Regulations for the Formation, Field-Exercise, and Movements, of His Majesty's Forces (1815). Dublin: A.B. King.

Scott, Winfield (1864). *Memoirs of Lieut.-General Scott*. New York, NY: Sheldon & Co.

Smyth, Alexander (1812). *Regulations for the Field Exercise, Manœuvres, and Conduct of the Infantry of the United States*. Philadelphia, PA: Anthony Finley.

Strother, D.H. (1847). *Illustrated Life of General Winfield Scott*. New York, NY: A.S. Barnes & Co.

Van Rensselaer, Solomon (1836). *A Narrative of the Affair of Queenston: In the War of 1812*. New York, NY: Levit, Lord & Co.

Wilkinson, James (1816). *Memoirs of My Own Times, Vol. 3*. Philadelphia, PA: Abraham Small.

Wool, John E. Letter to W.L. Stone dated September 13, 1838. In *The New York Public Library Bulletin* No. 9, 1905, pp. 120–22.

INDEX

References to illustrations are shown in **bold**.
References to plates are shown in **bold** with
caption pages in brackets, e.g. **38–39**, (40).